PARNASSUS BICEPS

Parnassus Biceps

or

Severall Choice Pieces of Poetry

by
ABRAHAM WRIGHT

1656

*together with pages from
British Library Additional MS 22608*

A facsimile edition
with introduction and indexes
by
Peter Beal

Scolar Press

The Introduction and Indexes © Peter Beal, 1990

Published by
SCOLAR PRESS
Gower House
Croft Road
Aldershot
Hants GU11 3HR
England

Gower Publishing Company
Old Post Road
Brookfield
Vermont 05036
USA

British Library Cataloguing in Publication Data
Parnassus biceps, or Severall choice pieces of poetry 1656:
   together with pages from British Library Additional
   MS 22608: a facsimile edition. – (English verse miscellanies
   of the 17th century)
   1. Poetry in English 1625–1702
   I. Wright, Abraham, *1611–1690* II. Series
   821.408

   ISBN 0–85967–782–6

Printed in Great Britain by
The Ipswich Book Company Ltd

Contents

General Editor's Foreword vii

Introduction ix

A Note on the Text xviii

Literature and References xix

Table of Contents xx

The Facsimile 2

Appendix 183

Index of Authors 194

Index of Titles 201

Index of First Lines 207

English Verse Miscellanies of the Seventeenth Century

Foreword by the General Editor

This series of facsimile editions is designed to make available texts of seventeenth-century English poetry that was commonly circulated in miscellanies, both manuscript and printed. The collections represented include familiar poems by many of the most celebrated names of the period, as well as much verse that is otherwise obscure or anonymous.

Limitations of format preclude detailed discussion of particular poems, authorship, dating, comparative texts and other subjects appropriate to elaborate critical editions. However, some relevant information is given, purely as a guide, in the editor's introduction and indexes. In the Table of Contents, any attribution which appears in the source is cited after the title of the poem within single inverted commas; this is followed, in square brackets, by the editor's own attribution, indicating the likely or generally accepted authorship. Uncertain or doubtful attributions which are known to occur in other sources are signalled '*attrib*'. Very brief outlines of the education and careers of identified or attributed authors are given in the Index of Authors.

For convenient reference, alphabetical Indexes of Titles and First Lines are also provided: titles according to exact wording of the original (ignoring definite and indefinite articles), and also according to the first adjective, noun or pronoun (following a preposition); first lines in modernized spelling with minimum punctuation.

Peter Beal

English Verse Miscellanies of the Seventeenth Century

Foreword by the General Editor

Introduction

Abraham Wright's miscellany *Parnassus Biceps* was published in London in 1656, evidently by 15 April (the date written in George Thomason's copy), having been entered in the Stationers' Register on 12 March. The printer, George Eversden, bookseller of St Paul's Church Yard, London, seems to have been more generally known for theological publications. The book is an essentially retrospective anthology of some ninety-four poems composed chiefly during the reigns of James I and Charles I. Wright's title page proclaims it to be a collection of verse 'Composed by the best Wits that were in both the Universities before their Dissolution': poems, that is to say, composed before the disruptions in the university life of Oxford and Cambridge brought about by the Civil War and ensuing Parliamentary Committees. In fact, the contents consist of verse almost entirely by Oxford men. The texts certainly derive from manuscript sources, although, as it happens, some of the poems had found their way into print in other publications. The book is essentially a printed version of what would otherwise be, for the most part, a fairly standard verse miscellany of a kind normally circulated at Oxford, before the Civil War, in manuscript form.

The compiler

Abraham Wright, who was born in London on 23 December 1611, was educated at Merchant Taylors' School and matriculated at St John's College, Oxford, on 13 November

1629. He was elected Fellow of his college in 1632, graduated
B.A. in 1633 and M.A. in 1637. On 27 September 1637 he
was ordained deacon by Francis White, Bishop of Ely, and
on 22 December 1639 John Bancroft, Bishop of Oxford,
ordained him priest. In August 1645 he was presented to the
vicarage of Oakham in Rutland by William Juxon, then
Bishop of London, who remained his constant patron.
Wright's staunch Royalist principles, however, precluded him
from taking the Solemn League and Covenant which was
necessary for him to receive Induction, and the Parliamentary
Commission also expelled him from his college fellowship.
He subsequently found employment as tutor to the son of Sir
James Grime (or Graham) at Peckham in Surrey until about
1655 when he moved to London, where he was chosen by the
parishioners of St Olave's in Silver Street to be their
'unofficial' minister for the next four years. It was here, while
he was 'one of the Cavalier Ministers of London' and, as
Anthony Wood says, not without 'his share in troubles' under
the Commonwealth, that he arranged the publication of
Parnassus Biceps. Following the Restoration, and despite
being offered the position of Chaplain to Elizabeth, Queen
of Bohemia, he took up possession of his living at Oakham.
A 'sober', 'reserv'd' and 'charitable' man, who resolutely
supported the Church of England, longed for 'Catholick
Unison and Harmony' in the Church and had little time for
Dissenters, Wright endeavoured to lead a quiet life with his
family, his garden and his parishioners until his death thirty
years later, on 9 May 1690.

Wright married twice. His first wife, Jane (née Stone) bore
him his elder son, James (1643–1713), and died in 1645. His
second wife, also Jane (née Wait), bore him a son, Richard
(*b.* 1666/7), and a daughter, Jane (*b.*1677). Wright's will made
solid and practical provisions for his family, including the
settlement of his estate at Manton in Rutland upon whichever
of his sons first married a woman worth 'seven hundred
pounds or more'. His beneficiaries also included the widows,
orphans and poor of his parish. According to Philip Bliss in
1820, Wright's son James published an elegy on him, *Verses*

anniversary to the venerable Memory of his ever honoured Father (London, 1690, 8vo), but no copy of this can be traced at present. A memorial plaque to Wright is still preserved at Oakham Parish Church, its barely discernible Latin inscription outlining his life and recording: *Piè & tranquillè expiravit.*

Wright was known from his Oxford days as an eloquent writer, orator and preacher. Because of this he secured the patronage of Bishop Juxon (whose love of 'soft Rhetorick' Wright praises in his poem on Juxon in *Parnassus Biceps*, p. 2) and he was chosen to deliver the speech welcoming Charles I to the new library at St John's on 30 August 1636. According to Wood, he wrote besides, as an undergraduate, 'a comical Entertainment called *The Reformation*, presented before the University at S. Johns Coll.', and he acted himself in George Wilde's comedy *Love's Hospital*, which was presented for the Royal visitors to the college on 30 August 1636. He wrote various poems in English, including lines printed in the Oxford miscellanies *Flos Britannicus* (1636) and *Horti Carolini Rosa Altera* (1640) and six poems incorporated (anonymously) in *Parnassus Biceps*. In 1637, being, as Wood says, 'an exact master of the Latine tongue, even to the nicest criticisme', he published under the title *Delitiae Delitiarum* an anthology of several hundred neo-Latin epigrams by some 120 continental Renaissance authors whose works were represented in the Bodleian Library (they include such writers as Pope Urban VIII, Theodore Beza, Jan Gruter, J. C. Scaliger, Hugo Grotius, Daniel Heinsius, Marius Bettinus, Jacobus Bidermanus, Balduinus Cabilliavus, Petrus Lotichius and Georgius Sabinus). This volume, which allegedly took three months to compile, was dedicated to Wright's contemporary at St John's, Dr William Haywood (1600?–63), William Laud's chaplain. Certain of Wright's earlier sermons, including one preached before the King at Christ Church and others preached at St Mary's, Oxford, and at St Paul's, London, were published in 1656 as *Five Sermons*. In 1661 he published *A Practical Commentary or Exposition upon the Book of Psalmes*, dedicated to the Baptist Viscount Camden and allegedly written to promote 'Union of Affections among Christians, as might prepare and incline them to submit to a General Council'. In the following year he published *A Practical Commentary or Exposition upon the Pentateuch*, an attempt 'to make our great Law-giver Moses altogether . . . applicable to the Life and Conversations of Christians' and dedicated to the Chief Justices of the realm. In 1668, under the pseudonym 'Abraham Philotheus' (meaning 'Lover of God'), his last publication appeared, entitled *Anarchie Reviving, or, the Good old Cause on the Anvil, being a Discovery of the present Design to retrive the late Confusions both of Church and State, in several Essays for Liberty of Conscience*. A vigorous political diatribe against extreme Dissenters, this was written, as the author himself notes (p. 73), in an uncharacteristically harsh vein: 'If you wonder at my style, as too biting for my temper; I alledge, that the Spirit of Meekness can be but of little use against a Party that wants Modesty'.

Wright's manuscripts, including further unpublished works (such as an account of public transactions from 1685 to 1690), passed to his son, the antiquary and miscellaneous writer James Wright, who is best remembered as probable author of the early history of the English stage *Historia Histrionica* (1699). Some of the latter's papers may have been destroyed in the fire at the Middle Temple in 1678. Many, however, were given before 1703 to the politician William Bromley (1664–1732) of Baginton, Warwickshire. Various of James Wright's manuscripts appeared in subsequent sales of the Bromley library (notably at Sotheby's on 25 November 1844 and 8 May 1903). Among the items dispersed, two of Abraham Wright's manuscripts appeared as lot 85 in the 1844 sale, when they were sold for 3s 6d to Taylor and acquired by the Oxford scholar Philip Bliss (1787–1857). One of these two works, Abraham Wright's Latin account of the trial of the Earl of Strafford, *Novissima Straffordii*, with an accompanying English translation by James Wright, was published by Bliss in *Historical Papers, Part I* (Roxburghe Club, Volume 62, London, 1846). The manuscript itself was sold in the Bliss sale at Sotheby's on 21 August 1858, lot 221, for 1s to Waller. The other manuscript by Abraham Wright which Bliss acquired was a compilation to which Wright's son James had given the title 'Excerpta quaedam per A.W. adolescentem. This manuscript was sold in the Bliss sale in 1858 as lot 220 (for 2s 6d to Boone) and is now in the British Library (Add. MS 22608). It comprises a 120-leaf quarto miscellany of extracts from six prose histories (by Bacon, Camden, Fuller, Henry Blount, William Martyn, Francis Godwin and Anthony Stafford) and from twenty-eight plays (by Shakespeare, Jonson, Beaumont and Fletcher, James Shirley, Henry Shirley, Davenant, Webster and Massinger), together with critical comments on those plays (see Appendix below). This miscellany was probably compiled circa 1640 and is entirely in Abraham Wright's own hand, as may be confirmed by a comparison with two surviving letters by him in the Leicestershire Record Office.

These various works give a sufficiently clear indication of Wright's literary tastes and inclinations, as well as of his High Church political and religious views. Wright's 'Genie', as Wood said, 'enclined him to Poetry and Rhetorick' and, at a time of upheaval, he remained passionately devoted to the ideals of 'Humane Learning' as practised at the Universities, not least because of the command of eloquence which they fostered. Wright's own keen sense of style is demonstrated, among other things, by his Novissima Straffordii, which is written 'in pure Latine and stile of Tacitus', and by his Five Sermons, which are written in 'Five several Styles, or Waies of Preaching' (namely, in imitation of Lancelot Andrewes, Joseph Hall, Jasper Mayne and William Cartwright, as also 'in the Presbyterian Way' and 'in the Independent Way'). The latter was published, Wright claimed in his preface, as a model to counteract the current abysmal and much complained-about standards of preaching under the Commonwealth, 'to shew the difference betwixt Universitie and Citie-breeding up of Preachers'. He gives an interesting illustration of the importance of scholarly accomplishments in rhetoric and oratory:

So should I see an English Clergie-man to equal at the least
the Jesuite or Capuchine, who by his exact skill in the Arts
and Oratorie can command a confused Rabble (met to see
an Interlude, or Mountebank) from their sport to a Sermon,
and change the Theater into a Church; having a greater
power over the passions of their Auditorie, then the Actor
hath upon the Stage; being able to turn even the Player
himself into a Monk, and the Mimical Jester into a religious
Votarie.

His surviving manuscript miscellany (Add. MS 22608), which
contains so many extracts from plays, as well as histories, was
evidently compiled in large part as a repository of memorable
phrases and expressions. Considerations of eloquence
consequently share equal prominence with those of 'plot' in
his remarks on particular dramatists. Thus, *Othello* and some
of Shirley's and Davenant's plays are complimented for their
'lines' and 'passages', while *Hamlet* and certain others by
Massinger and Fletcher are condemned because their 'lines'
are 'meane', 'plaine' or 'ordinary'. In this respect Wright was
here following a common practice of his period in compiling
a commonplace book as a rhetorical guide to be used for
reference and as a possible means of improving one's own
literary style. It was evidently used later also for the
instruction of his son, James, whose attention was directed
to particular expressions, authors or books by added
comments such as 'imitate him . . . take out of these some
sett expressions . . . and make common vse of them vpon
their several occas[ions]'. Judging by the catalogue
descriptions of certain of James Wright's own miscellanies
and commonplace books sold at Sotheby's on 8 May 1903,
James would appear to have followed in his father's footsteps.
James was obviously influenced by his father's dramatic tastes
as well: witness, for instance, the dialogue in his *Country
Conversations* (London, 1694, pp. 15–16), in which are
praised the 'Beauties of those [comedies] before the Wars
. . . [by] Ben. Johnson, Shakspear, Beaumont and Fletcher,
Messenger, Shirley, and Sir William Davenant'.

Contents

The ninety-four poems included in *Parnassus Biceps* may have been no more than a random selection of university poems which Abraham Wright happened to have at hand at a particular time, perhaps in one or more of his manuscript miscellanies. Certainly the volume amounts to an anthology no more distinguished in the quality of its verse than the average miscellany normally found in manuscript form in this period and is less distinguished than some. Nevertheless, Wright's preface makes it clear that he regarded the poems included as in some ways rhetorical models, worthy of imitation, and as representative of the cultural ideals he valued most. They are, he tells the reader, but 'some few drops of that Ocean of Wit, which flowed from those two brests of this Nation, the two Universities'. They derived from that pre-Civil War period when, as he nostalgically recalled, 'peace and plenty were the best Patriots and Maecenasses to great Wits' and before 'that Twin-Paradise [had] become desart'. It is characteristic of his interest in the type of poetry they represent, rather than in the particular poems themselves, that less than half a dozen of them are specifically assigned to their authors, and even Wright's own contributions are known only from Anthony Wood's testimony.

Cambridge men (such as Herrick, Randolph, Waller and Abraham Holland) account for no more than a small handful of the poems included, leaving the great majority by Oxford men. Of these the lion's share – including a number of poems by Richard Corbett, his chaplain William Strode, Henry King and William Cartwright – were written by Christ Church men. This proportion indeed reflects the kind of balance found in contemporary manuscript miscellanies produced at Oxford, for Christ Church – many of whose students traditionally came from Westminster School – was clearly a flourishing centre for the production and dissemination of poetry before the Civil War. No less than twenty-eight of the poems which appear in *Parnassus Biceps* can be found, for instance, in

Folger Shakespeare Library MS V. a. 97, an Oxford miscellany of the late 1630s probably associated with Christ Church, and comparable examples can be found elsewhere. Almost all the poems in *Parnassus Biceps* date from, and were chiefly circulated in, the period 1610–1640. Unless Donne's elegy 'The Anagram' (on p. 86) dates from the 1590s (as has sometimes been suggested, although, like 'The Autumnal' on p. 118, it is generally thought to date from the 1600s), the earliest dateable poem would appear to be the satire on the parsimonious Henry Sambourne (p. 22), who became High Sheriff of Oxfordshire in 1608, the very latest poem being the epithalamion on John Talbot and Elizabeth Kite (p. 55), who were married on 11 December 1653.

Although some of the poems reflect the controversies of the impending Civil War, and no poem is anything but wholly Royalist in sympathy, the favourite subject – for over thirty poems – is women, female beauty and the related joys and sorrows of earthly love, treated either lyrically or cynically, or (like many other subjects) as an opportunity for witty, elaborate and even bizarre conceits. Other characteristic themes and treatments include joyful celebrations of public events (such as Royal visits), satires on Puritan 'Zelots' (and, occasionally, on Roman Catholicism as well) and paeans in praise of wine, as well as lyrical and eulogistic exercises, sometimes marked by hyperbole or luxuriant metaphor, in honour of art (painting, stained glass, jewelry, needlework), poetry and music. Many of the poems thus celebrate aspects of civilized life which were hardly patronized by the Philistine Commonwealth. While the majority of poems reflect a sense of the enjoyment of life, that sense of mortality which is rarely absent for long from the minds of seventeenth-century poets manifests itself in, among other things, some fifteen epitaphs; nevertheless, they are, in effect, celebrations of those positive virtues which distinguished the lives of the various worthies whose deaths are lamented. For Wright, who speaks rapturously of Charles I's *Eikon Basilike* as 'A Book, where every leafe's a Library/Fill'd with choise Gems of th' Arts, Law, Gospel' (p. 54), *Parnassus Biceps* too was evidently considered to be in some measure a guide to wisdom and knowledge. The authors represented were, Wright declares in his preface, both poets and prophets, 'not onely in the ravishing expressions and extasies of amorous Composures and Love Songs; but in the more grave Dorick strains of sollid Divinity': they were poets attuned both to 'the sad note, and melancholy look of a disconsolate Elegy' and to 'those more sprightly jovial Aires of an Epithalamium, or Epinichion' and who were 'Priests, as well as Poets; who can teach you to pray in verse'. They represented the life of the spirit, of true learning and religion and of 'fancy', or imagination, before the lyre had been untuned and England's harmony reduced to discord.

It may be added that Wright showed neither more nor less interest than the average miscellany-compiler of his period in perfecting his texts, or in performing the function of an 'editor' in the modern sense, but simply offered to the printer those manuscript copies which he happened to have at hand, warts and all. His attitude in this respect is probably reflected in the Latin note which is appended to some (but not all) copies of his *Delitiae Delitiarum*, in which he claims to have spotted major printing errors but asks his reader to emend for himself less important, but more frequent, ones. Fortunately his texts seem, on the whole, with only occasional exceptions, to have been reasonably sound.

Peter Beal

A Note on the Text

The exemplar of *Parnassus Biceps* reproduced in the present facsimile edition is that in the British Library (pressmark E. 1679 (1)) once owned by George Thomason (*d.* 1666). Its collation is: 8^0. A–L^8 M^2. A1^r, title; A1^v blank; A2–A8^v preface (14pp.); text, pp. 1–163; p. [164] blank. It should be noted that what should be pages 90–96 are misnumbered as 91–97.

Literature and References

Arthur E. Case, *Bibliography of English Poetical Miscellanies
    1521–1750* (Oxford, 1935), No. 113.

Dictionary of National Biography ('Abraham Wright').

Arthur C. Kirsch, 'A Caroline Commentary on the Drama',
    Modern Philology, 66 (1968–9), 256–61.

James G. McManaway, '*Excerpta quaedam per A.W. adoles-
    centem*', *Studies in Shakespeare, Bibliography and Theater*
    (New York, 1969), pp. 279–91.

Falconer Madan, *Oxford Books*, 3 vols (Oxford, 1895–1931),
    III, No. 2294.

Parnassus Biceps, ed. G. Thorn-Drury (London, 1927).

The Visitation of the County of Rutland, 1681–1682,
    Publications of the Harleian Society, Volume 73 (London,
    1922), p. 7.

Anthony à Wood, *Athenae Oxonienses* [first published 1691–
    2], ed. Philip Bliss, 4 vols (London, 1813–20), IV, 275–8.

Abraham Wright, Last Will and Testament, signed on 28
    January '1685' (original: Public Record Office, PROB 10/
    1208, proved 31 May 1690; registered copy: PROB 11/399/
    82).

Abraham Wright, two autograph letters signed, one undated,
    the other dated 22 October 1661 (Leicestershire Record
    Office, DE 730/1, pp. 3 and 60).

*Information has also been kindly supplied, in private corres-
pondence, by the Rev. Canon Dr Alan A. Horsley, former
vicar of Oakham*

Table of Contents

page

The Temper. Upon Dr. Juxon Bishop of London [by
    Abraham Wright]   1
A Poem, In defence of the decent Ornaments of
    Christ-Church Oxon, occasioned by a Banbury
    brother, who called them Idolatries   3
An Elegie, Upon the death of Sir John Burrowes,
    Slaine at the Isle of Ree [by John Earles]   12
On a white blemish in his Mistresse eye [by Abraham
    Holland]   16
To Mr. Hammon Parson of Beudly For pulling down
    the May-pole [by Richard Corbett; also *attrib*. John
    Harris]   18
On Mr. Sambourne, sometime Sherife of
    Oxford-shire [by Benjamin Stone]   22
Upon the Sheriffs Beere [possibly part of previous
    poem]   23
A journey into France [by Thomas Goodwyn]   24
Ben: Johnson To Burlace [by Ben Jonson]   29
Upon the death of Prince Henry [by Henry King]   30
On the Bible [by William Strode]   31
Upon some pieces of work in York House [by William
    Lewis]   32
Sir Henry Wotton on Q: Elizabeth [by Sir Henry
    Wotton]   34
On the Princes birth [by James Shirley]   36
A Letter to his Mistresse [by William Strode]   39

On the Earle of Pembroke's Death [by Jasper Mayne; also *attrib.* John Earles]   40

Upon his chast Mistresse [by Thomas Randolph]   43

On a Painters handsome Daughter [by William Cartwright]   45

To Dr. Price writing Anniversaries on Prince Henry [by Richard Corbett]   46

A Reply upon an Answer to the former Copy [by Richard Corbett]   47

On a Lady that dyed of the small pox [by Richard Corbett]   48

Upon the Kings Returne to the City of London when he came last thether from Scotland and was entertained there by the Lord Mayor   50

Upon the Kings Book bound up in a Cover coloured with His Blood [by Abraham Wright]   54

Upon the Nuptials of John Talbot Esquire, and Mistresse Elizabeth Kite   55

Upon Aglaura Printed in Folio [by Richard Brome]   57

Venus lachrimans [by William Cartwright]   59

An Ode in the Praise of Sack   60

An Epitaph on some bottles of Sack and Claret laid in sand [by Robert Wild]   63

How to choose a Mistresse [*attrib.* John Donne]   64

Upon a Picture [by Sir Henry Blount]   64

On Ladies Attire [by Richard Corbett]   65

The Answer [*attrib.* John Grange]   66

On a Gentlewoman that had the Small-Pox [by William Strode]   67

On a faire Gentlewomans blistered lip [by William Strode]   67

To his Mistresse [compound of two poems by William Strode and Thomas Carew]   68

A lover to one dispraising his Mistresse [by Henry King]   70

On the death of a faire Gentlewomans Robin-redbrest   71

On the death of Sir Tho: Pelham [by William Strode]   72

Of Musick [by William Strode]   74

To his Mistresse [*attrib*. 'W.S.' and ‹William› Baker]   75
On a black Gentlewoman [by Walton Poole]   75
On a Gentlewoman walking in the Snow [by William
   Strode]   77
Upon one dead in the Snow [by William Browne]   78
On a woman dying in travell the child unborne [by
   William Browne]   79
On Man [by Henry King]   80
On F25aireford windows [by Richard Corbett]   81
On a Gentlewoman playing on the Lute [by William
   Strode]   82
On Love [*attrib*. ‹Sir John› Vaughan]   82
The Catholick [*attrib*. William Strode]   83
On Faireford windowes [by William Strode]   84
On the praise of an ill-favoured Gentlewoman [by
   John Donne]   86
Upon Heavens best Image, his faire and vertuous
   Mistresse M.S.   88
The black maid to the faire boy [by Henry Reynolds]   '91' [90]
His Answer [by Henry King]   '91' [90]
Verses sent to a Lady which she sending back unread,
   were returned with this inscription [by George
   Morley]   '92' [91]
The Verses [part of previous poem]   '93' [92]
The Nightingale [by George Morley]   '94' [93]
Barclay his Epitaph   '95' [94]
A welcome to Sack [by Robert Herrick]   '96' [95]
A Paradox on the praise of a painted face [*attrib*.
   William Baker, J‹ohn› D‹onne›, James Shirley]   97 *bis*
A Song [by William Strode]   100
Upon Mr. Hoptons death [by Henry Halswell]   101
On his Mistresse eye   102
To Dr. Griffith heald of a strange cure by Bernard
   Wright of Oxford [by William Strode]   104
The Liberty and Requiem of an imprisoned Royalist
   [by Sir Roger L'Estrange]   107
To his imperious Mistresse [by Alexander Brome]   110
On Dr. Ravis Bishop of London [by Richard Corbett]   112

TABLE OF CONTENTS

On Dr. Langton [by William Strode]   114
To the Bell-Founder of great Tom of Christ-Church
    in Oxford [*attrib*. Richard Corbett]   115
On a Gentleman, that kissing his Mistresse left blood
    upon her [by William Strode]   117
On an aged Gentlewoman [by John Donne]   118
On his Mistresse going to Sea [by Thomas Carey of
    the Bedchamber]   120
A Copy of Verses spoke to King Charles by way of
    entertainment when he was pleas'd to grace S. John's
    Colledge with his visit. 1636 [by Abraham Wright]   121
Upon the new Quadrangle of St. Johns Colledge in
    Oxford, built by the most Reverend Father in God
    the Lord Archbishop of Canterbury [by Abraham
    Wright]   122
Fortunes Legacy [by Martin Harvey]   124
Upon a Gentlewomans entertainment of him [by
    Abraham Wright]   126
To a black Gentlewoman Mistresse A.H. [by
    Abraham Wright]   128
To the Memory of Ben: Johnson [by Jasper Mayne]   129
An Answer to the Letter of the Cloake [by William
    Bond]   134
Loves Courtship [by William Cartwright]   136
Upon the death of the Lord Stafford, the last of his
    name [by William Cartwright]   137
Upon the same [by Richard Godfrey]   141
A Song of the Precise Cut [by William Strode]   143
Upon the Lady Paulets Gift to the University of
    Oxford: Being an exact piece of Needle-work
    presenting the whole story of the Incarnation,
    Passion, Resurrection, and Ascension of our
    Saviour [by William Cartwright]   146
On the same [by Edward Dalby]   148
On the same [by Thomas Gawen]   150
Against Ben: Johnson [by Owen Felltham]   154
Upon a Gentlewoman who broke her vow [by Henry
    King]   157

A Song upon a Winepot [*attrib.* 'N.N.' *et al.*]   158
To one married to an old man [by Edmund Waller]   159
A Song (I mean to sing of Englands fate)   159
Upon the Times [*attrib.* John Digby, first Earl of
   Bristol]   161
A double Chronogram (the one in Latine the other
   in the English of that Latine) upon the year 1642   161
On the Noble-mans Sons Cloak that refused to wear
   a Gown in Oxford   162
On Alma's voyce   163

Appendix

Five pages from British Library Additional MS 22608

[Facsimile text of *Parnassus Biceps*: – title page (1 p) + blank (1 p) + 'To the Ingenuous Reader' (14 pp) + 163 pages of text, 8vo-size]

Parnassus Biceps.

OR

Severall Choice Pieces

OF

POETRY,

Composed by the best WITS
that were in both the

Universities

BEFORE THEIR

DISSOLUTION.

With an Epistle *in the behalfe of
those now doubly secluded and sequestred
Members, by One who himselfe is gone.*

15. Aprill LONDON:
Printed for *George Eversden* at the Signe
of the *Maidenhead* in St. *Pauls*
Church-yard. 1656.

R

To the Ingenuous
READER.

SIR,

These leaves, present you
with some few drops
of that Ocean of Wit,
which flowed from those
two breasts of this Nation, the two U-
niversities; and doth now (the sluces
being puld up) overflow the whole
Lands; or rather like those Springs
of Paradice, doth water and enrich
the whole world; whilst the Foun-
tains themselves are dryed up, and
that Twin-Paradise become desart.
For then were these Verses Compa-
sed, when Oxford and Camebridge
were Universities, and a Colledge

A 2   *more*

more learned then a Town-Hall; when
the Buttery and Kitchin could speak
Latine, though not Preach; and the
very irrational Turnspits had so
much knowing modesty, as not to
dare to come into a Chappel, or to
mount any Pulpit but their own. Then
were these Poems writ, when peace
and plenty were the best Patriots
and Mæcenasses to great Wits;
when we could sit and make Verses
under our own Figtrees, and be in-
spired from the juice of our own
Vines: then, when it was held no
sin for the same man to be both a
Poet, and a Prophet; and to draw
predictions no lesse from his Verse,
then his Text. Thus you shall meet here
St. Pauls Rapture in a Poem, and
the fancy as high and as clear as
the third Heaven, into which
that

that *Apostle* was caught up : and this not onely in the ravishing expressions and extasies of amorous *Composures* and *Love Songs*; but in the more grave *Dorick* strains of sollid *Divinity* : *Anthems* that might have become *Davids Harpe*, and *Asaphs Quire*, to be sung, as they were made , with the *Spirit* of that chief *Musitian. Againe*, In this small *Glasse* you may behold your owne face, fit your own humors, however wound up and tuned ; whether to the sad note, and melancholy look of a disconsolate *Elegy* , or those more sprightly jovial *Aires* of an *Epithalamium*, or *Epinichion*. *Further*, would you see a *Mistresse* of any age, or face, in her created, or uncreated complexion : this mirrour presents you with more shapes then a *Conju-*

A 3   *rers*

rers *Glaſſe*, or a *Limners Pencil*. It
will alſo teach you how to court that
Miſtreſſe, when her very waſhings
and pargettings cannot flatter her;
how to raiſe a beauty out of wrinkles
four core years old, and to fall in love
even with deformity and uglineſſe.
From your *Miſtreſſe* it brings you to
your God; and (as it were ſome new
Maſter of the Ceremonies) inſtructs
you how to woe, and court him like-
wiſe; but with approaches and di-
ſtances, with geſtures and expreſſions
ſuitable to a Diety; addreſſes clothed
with ſuch a ſacred filial horror and
reverence, as may invite and embol-
den the moſt deſpairing condition of
the ſaddeſt gloomy Sinner; and withall
daſh out of countenance the greateſt
confidence of the moſt glorious Saint:
and not with that *Blaſph. mous* famili-
lia-

liarity of our new-enlightned and in-
spired men, who are as bold with the
Majesty and glory of that Light that
is unaprochable, as with their own
ignes fatui; and account of the third
Person in the blessed Trinity for no
more then their Fellow-Ghost; think-
ing him as much bound to them for
their vertiginous blasts and while-
winds, as they to him for his own most
holy spirit. Your Authors then of these
few sheets are Priests, as well as Po-
ets; who can teach you to pray in verse,
and (if there were not already too
much phantasticknes in that Trade)
to Preach likewise: while they turn
Scripture-chapters into Odes, and
both the Testaments into one book of
Psalmes: making Parnassus as sacred
as Mount Olivet, and the nine Muses
no lesse religious then a Cloyster of

A 4   Nuns

Nuns. But yet for all this I would not have thee, Courteous Reader, pass thy censure upon those two Fountains of Religion and Learning, the Universities, from these few small drops of wit, as hardly as some have done upon the late Assemblies three-half-penny Catechisme: as if all their publick and private Libraries, all their morning and evening watchings, all those pangs and throwes of their Studies, were now at length delivered but of a Verse, and brought to bed onely of five feet, and a Conceit. For although the judicious modesty of these Men dares not look the world in the face with any of Theorau Johns Revelations, or those glaring New-lights that have muffled the Times and Nation with a greater confusion and darknes, then ever benighted

ted

ted the world since the first *Chaos* :
yet would they please but to instruct
this ignorant *Age* with those exact
elaborate Pieces, which might reform
Philosophy without a *Civil War*, and
new modell even *Divinity* its selfe
without the ruine of either *Chuch*, or
State ; probably that most prudent
and learned *Order* of the *Church* of
Rome, the *Jesuite*, should not boast
more sollid, though more numerous
Volums in this kind. And of this
truth that *Order* was very sensible,
when it felt the rational *Divinity* of
one single *Chillingworth* to be an un-
answerable twelve-years-task for all
their *English Colledges* in *Chrisen-*
dome. And therefore that *Society* did
like its selfe, whe it sent us over a
War instead of an *Answer*, and pro-
ved us *Hereticks* by the sword : which

in

TO THE READER

in the first place was to Rout the Universities, and to teach our two Fountains of Learning better manners, then for ever hereafter to bubble and swell against the Apostolick Sea. And yet I know not whether the depth of their Politicks might not have advised to have kept those Fountains within their own banks, and there to have dammed them and choaked them up with the mud of the Times, rather then to have let those Protestant Streams run; which perchance may effect that now by the spreading Riverets, which they could never have done through the inclosed Spring: as it had been a deeper State-piece and Reach in that Sanedrim, the great Councell of the Jewish Nation, to have confined the Apostles to Jerusalem, and there to have muzzeld them

with

with Oaths, and Orders; rather then
by a fruitful Persecution to scatter a
few Gospel Seeds, that would spring
up the Religion of the whole world:
which had it been Coop'd within the
walls of that City, might (for all they
knew) in few years have expired and
given up the ghost upon the same Gol-
gotha with its Master. And as then e-
very Pair of Fishermen made a Church
and caught the sixt part of the world
in their Nets; so now every Pair of
Colledge-fellows make as many seve-
ral Universityes; which are truly so
call'd, in that they are Catholick, and
spread over the face of the whole
earth; which stands amazed, to see
not onely Religion, but Learning also to
come from beyond the Alpes; and that
a poor despised Canton and nook of the
world should contain as much of each

as all the other Parts besides. But them, *as* when our single *Jesus was* made an universall Saviour, and his particular Gospel the Catholick Religion; though that *Jesus* and this Gospel did both take their rise from the holy City; yet now no City is more unholy and infidel then that; insomuch that there is at this day scarce any thing to be heard of a Christ *at* Jerusalem, more then that such a one was sometimes there, nor any thing to be seen of his Gospel, more then a Sepulcher: just so it is here with us; where though both Religion and Learning do owe their growth, as well as birth, to those Nurseryes of both, the Universityes; yet, since the Siens of those Nurseryes have been transplanted, there's little remaines in them now (if they are not belyed) either of the old

Reli-

Religion and Divinity, more then its
empty Chair & Pulpit, or of the antient
Learning & Arts, except bare Schools,
and their gilded Superscriptions : so
far have we beggard our selves to en-
rich the whole world. And thus, In-
genuous Sir, have I given you the State
and Condition of this Poetick Miscel-
lany, as also of the Authors ; it being
no more then some few Slips of the best
Florists made up into a slender Gar-
land, to crown them in their Pilgri-
mage, and refresh thee in thine : if yet
their very Pilgrimage be not its selfe
a Crown equall to that of Confessors,
and their Academicall Dissolution a
Resurrection to the greatest temporall
glory : when they shall be approved of
by men and Angels for a chosen Ge-
neration, a Royal Priesthood, a pecu-
liar People. In the interim let this
com-

comfort be held out to you, our secluded
University-members, by him that is
none; (and therefore what hath been
here spoken must not be interpreted as
out of passion to my self, but meer zeal
to my Mother) that according to the
generally received Principles and Ax-
ioms of Policy, and the soundest Judg-
ment of the most prudential States-men
upon those Principles, the date of your
sad Ostracisme is expiring, and at an
end; but yet such an end, as some of
you will not embrace when it shall be
offered; but will chuse rather to con-
tinue Peripateticks through the whole
world, then to return, and be so in your
own Colledges. For as that great
Conncell of Trent had a Form and
Conclusion altogether contrary to the
expectation and desires of them that
procured it; so our great Conncels of
England

TO THE READER.

England (our late Parliaments) will
have such a result, and Catastrophe,
as shall no ways answer the Fasts and
Prayers, the Humiliations, and
Thanksgivings of their Plotters and
Contrivers: such a result I say, that
will strike a palsie through Mr. Pims
ashes, make his cold Marble sweat;
and put all those several Partyes, and
Actors, that have as yet appeard up-
on our tragical bloudy Stage, to an a-
mazed stand and gaze: when they
shall confess themselves (but too late)
to be those improvident axes and ham-
mers in the hand of a subtle Workman;
whereby he was enabled to beat down,
and square out our Church and State
into a Conformity with his own. And
then it will appeare that the great
Worke, and the holy Cause, and the
naked Arme, so much talked of for
these

*these fifteen years, were but the work,
and the cause, and the arme of that
Hand, which hath all this while rea-
ched us over the Alpes; dividing,
and composing, winding us up, and
letting us down, untill our very dif-
cords have set and tuned us to fuch
notes, both in our Ecclefiastical, and
Civill Government; as may sooneft
conduce to that most necessary Catho-
lick Unison and Harmony, which is
an essential part of Chrifts Church
here upon Earth, and the very Church
its selfe in Heaven. And thus far,
Ingenuous Reader, suffer him to be a
Poet in his Prediction, though not in
his Verse; who desires to be known
so far to thee, as that he is a friend to
persecuted Truth, and Peace; and
thy most affectionate Christian Ser-
vant,*

Ab: Wright.

University-Poems.

The Temper.
UPON
Dr JUXON
Bishop of LONDON.

Great Sir,

ANd now more great then when you were
Oth' Cabinet to your King, and Treasurer.
For then your acts were lock't from common view
Your life as Counsell being all Closet too ;
But now that Cabinet's opened, you doe passe
To th' world for the chiefe Jewel of the case :
Each vertue shines a severall glorious spark,
Which then were but one Diamond in the dark.
The Exchequer speaks your faith, this you to be
Astrue to the Counsell-board as Treasury ;

Which

Which care oth' civill good when they shall view
The houses will repeal their att for you ;
And in their graver policy debate (for th' State.
The cloak lesse fit for the Church, then th' gown
Next, to your place your low mind did accord
So well, you seem'd a Bishop and no Lord.
A Bishop such, as even the Scots to make
You theirs would arme, and a new Covenant take ;
Disband the Presbitery, and henceforth
Install you their sole Patriarch of the North.
Such power hath your soft Rhetorick, such awe
Your nod, and even your silence is a law ; (noyse
While others are not heard through their own
And by their speaking much have lost their voyce :
Thus those oth' starry Senate of the night (bright,
Which slowest tread their Orbs shine till most
And dart the strongest influx ; so conceal
The flints cold veins a fire ; such is the zeal
Of recluse Votaries, piercing the aire   (prayer.
And yet not heard, and such the Anchorites
Not like our modern Zelots, whose bare name
In Greek and Welch joyns language for a flame.
Gun-powder souls, whose Pulpit thoughts create
A calenture and feaver in the State ;
Whose plots and discipline are all fire, and shine
As hot, as if contrived under the line.
Your tempers cool and Northern, calculate
For the Miridian of this clime and State ;
And may be fitly stil'd the Courts pole-star,
Or honours best morall Philosopher :

So

So juſt your Sovereigne's, tis a hard thing
To ſay, which was the Biſhop, which the King.
This Temper took our State, by whom we ſee
The order queſtion'd yet the Biſhop free :
So that of all their Acts this ones moſt rare,
A Church-man ſcape and a Lord Treaſurer.

A Poem,

In defence of the decent Ornaments of Chriſt-
Church Oxon, occaſioned by a Banbury *bro-*
ther, who called them Idolatries.

YOu that prophane our windows with a tongue
Set like ſome clock on purpoſe to go wrong;
Who when you were at Service ſigh'd, becauſe
You heard the Organs muſick not the Dawes :
Pittying our ſolemn ſtate, ſhaking the head
To ſee no ruines from the flore to the lead :
To whoſe pure noſe our Cedar gave offence,
Crying it ſmelt of Papiſts frankincenſe :
Who walking on our Marbles ſcoffing ſaid
Whoſe bodies are under theſe Tombſtones laid :
Counting our Tapers works of darkneſſe ; and
Chooſing to ſee Prieſts in blew-aprons ſtand
Rather then in rich Coapes which ſhew the art
Of *Siſera's* prey Imbrodred in each part :
Then when you ſaw the Altars Baſon ſaid
Why's not the Ewer on the Cubboards head,

B 2   *Thinking*

Thinking our very Bibles too prophane,
Cause you nere bought such Covers in *Ducklane*.
Loathing all decency, as if yould have
Altars as foule and homely as a Grave.
Had you one spark of reason, you would finde
Your selves like Idolls to have eyes yet blind.
Tis onely some base niggard Heresie
To think Religion loves deformity.
Glory did never yet make God the lesse,
Neither can beauty defile holinesse.
Whats more magnificent then Heaven? yet where
Is there more love and piety then there.
My heart doth wish (wer't possible) to see
Pauls built with pretious stones and porphery:
To have our Halls and Galleries outshine
Altars in beauty, is to deck our swine
With Orient Pearl, whilst the deserving Quire
Of God and Angels wallow in the mire:
Our decent Copes onely distinction keep (sheep,
That you may know the Shepheard from the
As gaudy letters in the Rubrick shew
How you may holi-dayes from lay-dayes know:
Remember *Aarons* Robes and you will say
Ladies at Masques are not so rich as they.   (he
Then are th'Priests words like thunderclaps when
Is lightning like rayed round with Majesty.
May every Temple shine like those of *Nile*,
And still be free from Rat or Crocodile.   (be
But you will urge both Priest and Church should
The solemn patternes of humility.

                                        Doe

Doe not some boast of raggs ? Cynicks deride
The pomp of Kings but with a greater pride.
Meeknesse consists not in the cloaths but heart,
Nature may be vainglorious well as art ;
We way as lowly before God appear
Drest with a glorious pearl as with a tear ;
In his high presence where the Stars and Sun
Doe but Ecclipse ther's no ambition.
You dare admit gay paint upon a wall,
Why then in glasse that heid Apocriphall?
Our bodies Temples are : look in the eye
The window, and you needs must pictures spye ;
Moses and *Aaron* and the Kings armes are (were.
Daubed in the Church when you the Warden
Yet you nere find for Papist : shall w e say
Banbury is turnd *Rome*, because we may
See the holy Lamb and Christopher ? nay more
The Altar stone set at the Tavern doore ?
Why can't the Oxe then in the nativity
Be Imagd forth, but Papists Bulls are nigh?
Our pictures to no other end are made
Then is your Time and sith your death and spade ;
To us they'r but mementoes, which present,
Christ best, except his Word and Sacrament.
If 'twere a sin to set up Imagry,
To get a Child were flat Idolary.
The modells of our buildings would be thus
Directions to our houses, ruines to us.
Hath not each creature which hath daily birth
Something which resembles Heaven or Earth ?

Suppose

Suppose some ignorant Heathen once did bow
To Images, may we not see them now ?
Should we love darknesse and abhor the Sun
Cause Persians gave it adoration?
And plant no Orchards, because apples first
Made *Adam* and his lineall race accurst ?
Though wine for *Bacchus*, bread for *Ceres* went,
Yet both are now used in the Sacrament.
What then if these were Popish reliques ? few
Windowes are elsewhere old but these are new,
And so exceed the former, that the face
Of those come short of the outside of our glass ;
Colours are here mix'd so, that Rainbows be
(Compared) but clouds without variety.
Art here is Natures envy : this is he,
Not *Paracelsus*, that by Chymistry
Can make a man from ashes, if not dust,
Producing off-springs of his mind not lust.
See how he makes his maker, and doth draw
All that is meant ith' Gospel, or ith' Law :
Looking upon the Resurrection
Me thoughts I saw the blessed vision,
Where not his face is meerly drawn but mind,
Which not with paint but oile of gladness shind :
But when I viewed the next pane, where we have
The God of life transported to his grave,
Light then is dark, all things so dull and dead;
As if that part of the window had been lead.
Jonas his whale did so mens eyes befool (School.
That they'd have begd him for th' Anatomy

                                        That

That he faw Ships at *Oxford* one did fwear,
Though His yet will Barges hardly bear.
Another foon as he the trees efpied
Thought them i'th Garden on the other fide.
See in what ftate(though on an Affe)Chrift went,
This fhews more glorious then the Parliament.
Then in what awe *Mofes* his rod doth keep
The Seas,as if a froft had glaz'd the deep ;
The raging waves are to themfelves a bound ,
Some cry help help or horfe and man aredrownd.
Shadows doe every where for fubftance paffe,
You'd think the fands were in a houre-glaffe.
You that do live with Chirurgeons,have you feen
A fpring of blood forth from a fwelling vein ?
So from a touch of *Mofes* rod doth jump
A Chataract, the rock is made a pump :
At fight of whofe oreflowings many get
Themfelves away for fear of being wet.
Have you beheld a fprightfull Lady ftand
To have her frame drawn by a painters hand ?
Such lively look and prefence, fuch a dreffe
King *Pharoahs* Daughters Image doth expreffe;
Look well upon her Gown and you will fwear
The needle not the pencill hath been there :
At fight of her fome gallants doe difpute
Whether ith' Church 'tis lawfull to falute.
Next *Jacob* kneeling, where his Kids-fkins fuch
As it may well cofen old *Ifaacs* touch :   (bout
A Shepheard feeing how thorns went round a-
Abrahams ram,would needs have helpt it out.

B 4   Behold

Behold the Dove defcending to infpire
The Apoftles heads with cloven tongues of fire,
And in a fuperficies there youle fee
The groffe dimentions of profundity :
Tis hard to judge which is beft built and higher
The arch-roofe in the window or the Quire.
All beafts as in the Ark are lively done,
Nay you may fee the fhadow of the Sun.
Upon a landskip if you look a while
Youle think the profpect at leaft forty mile.
There's none needs now goe travell, we may fee
At home *Jerufalem* and *Nirevy* ;
And *Sodome* now in flames : one glance will dart
Farther then Lynce with *Galilaus* art.
Seeing *Eliahs* Chariot, we feare
There is fome fiery prodigy in the aire.
When Chrift to purge his Temple holds his whip
How nimbly huckfters vvith their baskets skip.
St. *Peters* fifhes are fo lively wrought,   (caught.
Some cheapen them and ask when they were
Here's motion painted too: Chariots fo faft
Run, that they're never gone though always paft.
The Angels with their Lutes are done fo true,
We doe not onely look but hearken too,
As if their founds were painted : thus the wit
Of the pencil hath drawn more then there can fit.
Thus as (in Archimedes fphear) you may
In a fmall glaffe the univerfe furvey :
Such various fhapes are too ith' Imagry
As age and fex may their own features fee.

                                        But

But if the window cannot shew your face
Look under fret the Marble is your glasse,
Which too for more then Ornament is there
The stones may learn your eyes to shed a tear :
Yet though their lively shadows delude sence
They never work upon the conscience ;
They cannot make us kneel ; we are not such
As think theres halfome in their kisse or touch,
That were grosse superstition we know ;   (toe.
There is no more power in them then the Popes
The Saints themselves for us can doe no good,
Muchlesse their pictures drawn in glass and wood,
They cannot seale, but since they signifie
They may be worthy of a cast oth' eye,
Although no worship : that is due alone
Not to the Carpenters but Gods own Sonne :
Obedience to blocks deserves the rod ;
The Lord may well be then a jealous God.
Why should not Statues now be due to *Paul*,
As to the *Cæsars* of the Capitall.
How many Images of great heires, which
Had nothing but the sin of being rich,
Shine in our Temples ? kneeling alwayes there
Where when they were alive they'd scarce appear.
Yet shall Christs Sepulcher have nere a Tomb ?
Shall every Saint suffer *John Baptists* doom ?
No limb of *Mary* stand ? must we forget
Christs crosse as soon as past the Alphabet ? (who
Shall not their heads have room in the window
Founded our Church and our Religion too ?
                                        We

We know that Gods a Spirit, we confesse
Thoughts cannot comprehend his name, muchlei's
Can a small glasse his nature : but since he
Vouchsaf'd to suffer his humanity,
Why may not we(onely to puts in mind (shrind?
Of his Godhead) have his manhood thus en-
Is our Kings person lesse esteemd because
We read him in our Coynes as well as Laws ?
Doe what we can, whether we think or paint,
All Gods expressions are but weak and faint.
Yet spots in Globes must not be blotted thence
That cannot shew the worlds magnificence.
Nor is it fit we should the skill controul
Because the Artist cannot draw the soul.
Cease then your railings and your dullcomplaints;
To pull down Galleries and set up Saints
Is no impiety : now we may well
Say that our Church is truely visible :
Those that before our glasse scaffolds prefer,
Would turne our Temple to a theater.
Windows are Pulpits now ; though unlearnd, one
May read this Bibles new Edition.
Instead of here and there a verse adornd
Round with a lace of paint, fit to be scornd
Even by vulgar eyes, each pane presents   (tents,
Whole chapters with both comment and con-
The cloudy mysteries of the Gospel here
Transparent as the Christall doe appear.
Tis not to see things darkly through a glasse,
Here you may see our Saviour face to face.

And

And whereas Feasts come seldome, here's descride
A constant Christmas, Easter, Whitsontide.
Let the deafe hither come ; no matter though
Faiths sence be lost, we a new way can shew :
Here we can teach them to believe by the eye;
These silenced Ministers doe edify :
The Scriptures rayes contracted in a Glasse
Like Emblems doe with greater vertue passe.
Look in the book of Martyrs and youle see
More by the Pictures then the History.
That price for things in colours oft we give (live.
Which wee'd not take to have them while they
Such is the power of painting that it makes
A loving sympathy twixt men and snakes.
Hence then *Pauls* doctrin may seem more divine,
As Amber through a Glasse doth clearer shine.
Words passe away, as soon as heard are gone ;
We read in books what here we dwell upon,
Thus then there's no more fault in Imagry
Then there is in the Practise of piety,
Both edifie : what is in letters there
Is writ in plainer Hierogliphicks here.
Tis not a new Religion we have chose ;
Tis the same body but in better cloaths.   (pray
Youle say they make us gaze when we should
And that our thoughts doe on the figures stray :
If so, you may conclude us beasts, what they
Have for their object is to us the way.
Did any ere use prospectives to see
No farther then the Glasse : or can there be

                                        Such

Such lazy travellers, so given to sin,
As that theyle take their dwelling at the Inne.
A Christians sight rests in Divinity,
Signes are but spectacles to help faiths ey ,
God is the Center : dwelling one these words,
My muse a Sabbath to my brain affords.
If their nice wits more solemn proof exact,
Know this was meant a Poem not a Tract.

An ELEGIE,

Upon the death of Sir John Burrowes,
Slaine at the Isle of Ree.

OH wound us not with this sad tale, forbear
To press our grief too much, we cannot hear
This all at once, such heavy newes as these
Must be sunk gently into us by degrees :
Say *Burrowes* is but hurt, let us disgest
This first, then try our patience for the rest.
Practise us first in lighter griefes, that we
May grow at last strong for this Tragedy.
Doe not speak yet he's slaine, or if he be
Speak't in a whisper or uncertainty,
As some new unauthoriz'd buzze without
Reason or warrant to confirme our doubt.
Come tis not so, tis but some flying talk
Newes lately vented in the audacious walk,

Some

Some lye thats drapt in *Pauls* to ftur our fears,
And gatherd by the bufie credulous eares. (there
Will you believe ought comes from thence ? why
The Forts furrendred, and the Rochellere
Sworne Euglifh, *Tillyes* flaine, the hoftile Kings
Clofed in our fiege, with fuch prodigious things,
Which your perfwaded vulgar takes and fends
Abroad as tokens to their country friends.
Are all thefe wonders falfe ? and onely this
True mongft fo many impoffibilities ?
Where truth is worfe then any forgery
There we may curfe his mouth that doth not lye,
When fame goes off with fuch a black report
Worfe then the murthering Canon from the fort.
Worfe then the fhot that killd him, for but one
Was killd with that, this kills a Nation.
Ile not believe it yet, doe we not know
An envious murder fam'd him dead ere now ;
Receiv'd went into Ballads and almoft
Clap'd in Caranto's upon every poft :
Why fhould he not now dye in jeft as then,
And we as haply be mock'd agen ?
But tis too certaine, here his Coarfe we have
Come ore to prove his death and ask a Grave,
A Grave for his good fervice : onely thus
Muft we reward thee that waft flaine for us,
To mourn and bury thee ? and would our fears
As foon were clos'd too as thy duft and tears.
I would thou mightft dye wholly here, and be
Forgotten, rather then our mifery

Should

Should urge thy fresh remembrance, and recall
Our sorrows often to lament thy fall,
When we shall say hereafter, tis well seen
Burrowes is dead else this had never been.
Why did we thus expose thee, whats now all
That Illand to requite thy Funerall ;   (lye
Though thousand troops of murdered French doe
It may revenge, it cannot satisfie: (done
They are before hand still, and when we have
Our worst we are loosers though theFort be won:
Our conquerers now will weep, whentheyshallsee
This price too dear to buy a victory :
He whose brave fire gave heat to all the rest
That dealt his spirits in each English breast ;
From whose divided vertues you might take
So many Captaines out and fully make   (which
Them each accomplisht with those parts the
Did joyntly his rare furnish'd soule enrich :
He whose command was ore himselfe more high
And strictly soure then ore his company :
Not rashly valiant nor yet fearfull wise,
His flame had counsell in't, his fury eyes,
Not struck with courage at the drums proud beat
Or made fierce onely by the Trumpets heat :
When even pale hearts above their pitch doe fly
And for a while doe mad it furiously :
His rage was temper'd well, no fear could dant
His reason his cold blood was valiant.
Alasse those vulgar praises injure thee,
Which now a Poet would as plenteously

                                        Give

Give some boy souldier, one that nere knew more
Then the fine Scabbard and the Scarfe he wore.
And we can pitch no higher ; thou haft outdone
So much our fancy and invention,
It cannot give thee ought. He that of thee
Shall write but halfe seems to write Poetry :
It is a ftrong line here to fpeak yet true,
Hyperboles in others is thy due.
Suffice it that thou wert our Armies all;   (pall
Whofe well tryed name did more the French ap-
Then all theirwants could do, whofe inward dread
Famifh'd them more in courage then in bread :
And we may make't a Queftion, whether moft
Befiegd their Caftle, *Burrowes*, or our Hoft.
Now let me blame thy vertue, it was this
Took thee from us and not our enemies.
Whilft thy unwearied toyle no refpite takes
And thinks reft floath, and with parpetual wakes
Continueft night with day and day with night ;
Thou waft more ventrous when thou didft not fight.
This did expofe thee to their fraud and mark ;
They durft not feize upon thee but ith' dark :
The coward bullet that fo oft before
Waved thy bold face and did fear thee more
Then thou feardft it, now by its errour is
Aimed too too fure: There was no light to miffe.
Thus fell our Captaine, and the found he's dead
Has fallen as deep; and like that fatall lead
Lies cold on us. Yet this thy honour be,
Thy hurts our wound, thy death our mifery.

Not

Not as the mourning of a private fate
But as some ruine had befallen the State :
The Fleet had been miscarried, *Denmark* tane
Or the Palatinate been lost againe.
So we with down-cast looks astonish'd quite
Receiv'd this not as newes but as a fright :
So we relate thy death, whilst each man here
Contributes to this publick losse a teare :
Whilst Fathers tell their children this was he ;
And they hereafter to posterity   (old
Range with those Forces that scourg'd *France* of
Burrowes and *Talbots* name together told.
VVhilst we ad this to our quarrel, and now more
Fight to revenge thee then our Land before.

On a white blemish in his
Mistresse eye.

IF there be haply any man that dares
Think that the blemish in the Moon impaires
Her modest beauty : He may be so farre
From right, as he that thinks a Swan may marre
A Christall stream, or Ivory make a smutch
Fairely enameld in a piece of touch.
He that thinks so may as well entertaine
A thought, that this faire snowie Christall staine,
Which (beautious Mistres) late usur p'd your eye,
Hath done your Heavenly face some injury

                                        He

He that thinks so nere let him have the blisse
To steale from your sweet lips a Nectar kisse.
Believe me (faire) and so you may, my duty
Is to observe left on your spotlesse beauty
The least wrong makes assault, it gives like grace
Being white with the black moal on *Venus* face;
Yea *Venus* happily envied your sight
Which wont to dazle her inferiour light,
So put out th' one eye cause it proudly strove
With her which most should kindle men in love,
Yet t'other to extinguish she forbore
Least then like *Cupid* you had wounded more.
If you will have me nature search, and tell you
What was the cause that this fair blot befell you:
It may be this, your dainty living torch
Which wont the greedy amorous eye to scorch
With a sweet murthering flame, when it couldnot
For greif of so much slaughter it grew pale: (wail
It may be these two dainty stars in lew
Oth' grace which they from one another drew,
(Kind twins) would needs like *Castor* and his bro-
Die in their turns so to enrich each other: (ther
Or whether 'twere that *Cupid* in his flight
Being drawn by such a most imperious light:
Refusing all beds else doth sleeping lye
White naked boy in your white spotted eye.
Or thus: Heaven seeing a sun in each your eye
Put out the one to scape a Prodigie;
Yet double grace from hence your beauty won
Now you have a pale Moon and glistering Sun.

C   Nor

Nor think your beauty now difgrac'd becaufe
You have but one eye, believe me natures Laws
(Being her felfe but one) admit no ftore
In perfect things : there's one Sun and no more,
Unleffe't be your left eye ; nor Moons more be,
Unleffe that eye make a plurality :
Which Moon-like fpotted is : the worlds but one :
The perfect gem is call'd an union :
One Earth there is, one Ocean, and the Gods
Joy not in equall numbers, but in odds.
To perfect all this, you my mufe affures
There's ftill one beauty in the world, thats yours.

To Mr. Hammon *Parfon of* Beudly
For pulling down the *May* pole.

THe mighty zeal which thou haft late put on ;
Neither by Prophet nor by Prophets fon
As yet prevented, doth tranfport me fo
Beyond my felfe, that though I nere could go
Far in a Verfe, and have all rimes defied
Since *Hopkins* and good *Thomas Sternhold* died,
Except it were the little paines I took
To pleafe good people in a Prayer-book
That I fet forth, or fo : yet muft I raife
My fpirits for thee, who fhall in thy praife
Gird up her loyns and furioufly runne
All kind of feet but Satans cloven one.

                                        Such

Such is thy zeal, so well thou dost expresse it
That wer't not like a charme I'd say God blesse it.
I needs must say it is a spirituall thing
To raile against the Bishop and the King :
But these are private quarrells, this doth fall
Within the compasse of the Generall.
Whether it be a Pole painted or wrought,
Far otherwise then from the wood'twas brought:
Whose head the Idol-makers hand doth crop ;
Where a prophane bird towring on the top
Looks like the Calfe in *Horeb*, at whose root
The unyoakt youth doth exercise his foot :
Or whether it preserves its boughs befriended
By neighbouring bushes and by them attended,
How canst thou chuse but seeing it complaine
That *Baals* worshap'd in the Groves againe :
Tell me how curst an egging with a sting
Of lust doe these unwily dances bring,
The simple wretches say they mean no harme
They don't indeed, but yet those actions warme
Our purer blood the more : For Satan thus
Tempts us the more that are more righteous.
Oft hath a Brother most sincerely gone
Stifled with zeal and contemplation,
When lighting on the place where such repaire
He views theNimph and is clean out in his prayer:
Oft hath a Sister grounded in a truth,
Seeing the jolly carriage of the youth,
Been tempted to the way thats broad and bad;
And wert not for our private pleasures, had

Re

Renounced her little ruffe and goggle eye
And quit her selfe of the fraternity.
What is the mirth ? what is the mellody
That sets them in this Gentiles vanity ?
When in our Synagogues we raile at sin,
And tell men of the faults that they are in,
With hand and voyce so following our theams
That we put out the sides men in their dreams :
Sounds not the Pulpit then which we belabor
Better and holier then doth a Tabor ;
Yet such is unregenerate mans folly,
He loves the wicked noyse, and hates the holy.
If the sins sweet enticing, and the blood
Which now begins to boyl, have thought it good
To challenge liberty and recreation
Let it be done in holy contemplation ;
Brother and Sister in the field may walk,
Beginning of the holy word to talk,
Of *David* and *Uriahs* lovely wife
Of *Thamar* and her lustfull Brothers strife,
Then underneath the hedge that is the next
They may sit down and so act out the Text.
Nor doe we want, how ere we live austere,
In winter Sabbath nights some lusty cheare ;
And though the Pastors grace which oft doth hold
Halfe an houre long make the provision cold,
We can be merry thinking nere the worse
To mend the matter at the second course ;
Chapters are read and Hymns are sweetly sung
Joyntly commanded by the nose and tongue :

                              Then

Then on the word we diverfly dilate
Wrangling indeed for heat of zeale, not hate,
When at the length an unappeafed doubt
Fiercely comes in, and then the lights go out.
Darkneffe thus makes our peace, and we containe
Our fiery fpi its till we meet againe :
Till then no voyce is heard, no tongue does go
Unleffe a tender Sifter fhreek or fo.
Such fhould be our delights grave and demure,
Not fo abominable, and impure
As thofe thou feekft to hinder : but I fear
Satan will be too ftrong, his kingdomes there.
Few are the righteous, nor dee I know
How we this Idol here fhall overthrow,
Since our fincereft Patron is deceaf'd
The number of the righteous is decreaf'd :
But we doe hope thefe times will on and breed
A faction mighty for us. For indeed
We labour all, and every Sifter joynes
To have regenerate babes fpring from our loyns :
Befides what many carefully have done
To get the unrighteous man a righteous fon.
Then ftoutly on, let not thy flocks range lewdly
In their old vanities, thou lamp of *Bendly.*
One thing I pray thee ; doe not fo much thirft
After Idolatries laft fall, but firft
Follow thy fuite more clofe, let it not go
Till it be thine as thou wouldft have't : for fo
Thy fucceffors upon the fame entaile
Hereafter may take up the Whitfun-ale.

On Mr. Sambourne, *sometime Sherife of* Oxford-*shire.*

Fie, Schollers, fie, have you such thirsty souls
To swill, quaffe, and carouse in *Samborns* bouls.
Tell me, mad youngsters, what doe you believe
It cost good *Sambourne* nothing to be Sheriffe ?
To spend so many beeves, so many weathers,
Maintaine so many Caps, so many Feathers.
Againe is malt so cheap, this pinching year,
That you should make such havock of his bear :
I hear you are so many, that you make
Most of his men turne Tapsters for your sake.
And that when he even at the Bench doth sit,
You snatch the meat from off the hungry spit :
You keep such hurly burly, that it passes,
Ingurgitating sometimes whole halfe glasses.
And some of you, forsooth, are grown so fine,
Or else so saucy, as to call for wine ;
As if the Sheriffe had put such men in trust,
As durst draw out more wine then needs they must.
In faith, in faith, it is not well my Masters,
Nor fit that you should be the Shrieffs tasters.
It were enough, you being such gormondizers,
To make the Shrieffs henceforth turn arrant misers
                                        Remove

Remove the Size, to *Oxfords* foul difgrace,
To *Henly* on the Thames, or fome fuch place.
He never had complained had it been
A petty Ferkin, or a Kilderkin :
But when a Barrel daily is drunk out,
My Mafters, then tis time to look about.
Is this a lye ? trow ye, I tell you no,
My Lord High-Chancelor was informed fo.
And oh, what would not all the bread in Town
Suffice to drive the Sheriffs liquor down :
But he in hampers muft it from hence bring ;
Oh moft prodigious, and moft monftrous thing !
Upon fo many loaves of home-made bread,
How long might he and his two men have fed ?
He would no doubt the poor they fhould be fed
With the fweet morfe' , of his broken bread :
But when that they poor foules for bread did call,
Anfwer was made, the Schollers eate up all :
And when for broken bear, they crav d a cup,
Anfwer was made, the Schollers drunk it up.
And thus I know not how they change the name,
Cut did the deed, and long-tale bore the blame.

Upon the Sheriffs Beere.

OUr *Oxford* Sheriffe of late is grown fo wife,
As to reprieve his Beere till next Affize :
Alaffe twas not fo ftrong, twas not fo heady,
The Jury fate and found it dead already.

A

A journey into France.

I Went from *England* into *France*,
Not for to learn to sing or dance,
        Nor yet to ride nor sence.
Nor yet did goe like one of those,
That thence returne with halfe the nose
        They carried from hence.
But I to *Paris* rode along,
Much like *John Dory* in the song,
        Upon a holy tide.
I on an ambling Nagge did get,
I trust he is not paid for yet,
        And spur'd him on each side.
And to St. *Dennis* first we came,
To see the sights of *Nostredam*,
        The man that shewes them snuffles.
Where who is apt for to believe,
May see our Ladies right arme sleeve,
        And eke her old pantafles.
Her brest, her milk, her very gown,
That she did weare in *Bethlem* Town,
        When in the Inne she lay.
No Carpenter could by his trade
Gaine so much coyn as to have made
        A Gown of so rich stuffe.
           Yet

Yet they poor fooles think't worth their credit,
They must believe old *Joseph* did it,
    Cause he deserv'd enough.
There is one of the Crosses Nailes,
Which who so sees his Bonnet vailes,
    And if he will may kneel.
Some say tis false twas never so ;
Yet feeling it thus much I know,
    It is as true as steel.
There is the Lanthorn which the *Jewes*,
When *Judas* led them forth did use,
    It weighs my weight down right.
But to believe it you must think,
The *Jewes* did put a candle in't,
    And then twas wondrous light
There's one Saint there hath lost his nose,
Another his head, but not his toes,
    His elbow and a thumb.
But when we had seen these holy rags,
We went to the Inne and took our Nags,
    And so away did come.
We came to *Paris* on the *Sene*,
Tis wondrous faire, but nothing cleane,
    Tis *Europes* greatest Town.
How strong it is I need not tell it,
For all the world may easily smell it,
    That walk it up and down.

       There

There many strange things are to see,
The Pallace, the great Gallery
                    The Pallace doth excell.
The New-bridge, and Statues there :
At *Nostredam* St. *Christopher,*
                    The Steeple bears the bell.
For learning the University ;
And for old cloths the Frippery,
                    The house the Queen did build.
St. *Innocents* whose earth devours
Dead corps in four and twenty hours,
                    And there the King was kil'd.
The Basteel, and St. *Dennis* street,
The Shatteet just like *London* Fleet,
                    The Arsenall no toy.
But if you'l see the prettiest thing,
Go to the Court and see the King,
                    Oh tis a hopefull boy.
He is of all his Dukes and Peers,
Reverencd for his wit and years :
                    Nor must you think it much.
For he with little switch can play,
And can make fine durt Pies of clay,
                    Oh never King made such.
A Bird that can but kill a fly,
Or prate, doth please his Magesty,
                    Tis known to every one.
The Duke of *Guise* gave him a Parrot,
And he had twenty Cannons for it,
                    For his great Gallioone.
                    Oh

Oh that I ere might have the hap
To get that Bird which in the Map
            Is call'd the *Indian* Duck ;
I'd give it him, and hope to be
As great as *Guise* or *Liciny,*
            Or elfe I had bad luck.
Birds about his Chamber ftand,
And he them feeds with his own hand ;
            Tis his humility :
And if they doe want any thing,
They need but whiftle for their King,
            And he comes prefently.
But now for thefe good parts he muft
Needs be inftil'd *Lewis* the juft,
            Great *Henryes* lawfull heire.
When to his ftile to adde more words,
They had better call him King of Birds,
            Then of the loft *Navarre.*
He has befides a pretty firke,
Taught him by nature how to work
            In Iron with much eafe :
Sometimes into the Forge he goes,
And there he knocks, and there he blows,
            And makes both locks and keys.
Which puts a doubt in every one,
Where he be *Mars* or *Vulcans* fon ;
            Some few believe his mother,
Yet let them all fay what they will,
I am refolv'd and doe think ftill,
            As much the one or t'other.
                The

The people don't diflike the youth,
Alleging reafons. For in truth
   Mothers fhould honoured be.
Yet others fay he loves her rather,
As well as ere fhe lov'd his Father,
    And thats notorioufly.
His Queen a little pretty wench,
Was born in *Spaine*, fpeaks little *French*,
   Nere like to be a Mother :
For her inceftuous houfe could not
Have children unleffe they were begot
   By Uncle or by Brother.
Now why fhould *Lewis* being fo juft,
Content himfelfe to take his luft,
   With his *Licina's* mate :
And fuffer his little pretty Queen,
From all her race that ere has been
   So to degenerate.
Twere charity for to be known
To love ftrange children as his own ;
   And why it is no fhame :
Unleffe he yet would greater be,
Then was his Father *Henry*,
   Who fome thought did the fame

        Ben:

BEN: JOHNSON

To Burlace.

WHy though I be of a prodigious wall,
I am not so voluminous and vast
But there are lines wherewithIm ay be embrac'd.
Tis true, as my womb swells, so my backstoops,
And the whole lump grows round, deform'd and
But yet the tun of *Heidleb:* has hoops. (droops;
You are not tyed by any Painters Law,
To square my circle, I confesse, but draw
My *superficies*, that was all you saw:
Which it in compasse of no art it came
To be describ'd, but by a Monagram,
With one great blot you have drawn me as I am.
But whilst you curious were to have it be
An Archetype for all the world to see,
You have made it a brave peece, but not like me.
Oh had I now the manner, mastery, might,
Your power of handling shadow, aire, and sprite,
How I could draw, behold, and take delight;
But you are he can paint, I can but write,
A Poet hath no more then black and white,
Nor has he flattering colours, orfalse light.

Yet

Yet when of friendship I would draw the face,
A letterd mind, and a large heart would place
To all posterity, I would write *Burlace*.

Upon the death of
Prince HENRY.

Keep station nature, and rest Heaven sure
On thy supporters shoulders, lest past cure
Thou dash'd by ruine fall with a great weight;
Twill make thy Basis shrink, and lay thy height
Low as the Centre. Death and horror wed
To vent their teeming mischiefe : *Henryes* dead.
Compendious eloquence of death, two words
Breath stronger terror then plague, fire, or swords
Ere conquerd. Why, tis Epitaph and Verse
Enough to be prefixt on natures Herse
At Earths last dissolution. Whose fall
Will be lesse griveous, though more Generall.
For all the woe ruine ere buried,
Lies in this narrow compasse : *Henries* dead.

On

On the *BIBLE.*

BEhold this little Volume here enrold,
Tis the Almighties Prefent to the world.
Hearken Earth, Earth : Each fenfleffe thing can
His makers thunder, though it want an eare. (hear
Gods word is fenior to his work ; nay rather
If rightly weighd, the world may call it Father.
God fpake, twas done : this great foundation
Was but the makers exhalation,
Breathd out in fpeaking. The leaft work of man
Is better then his word ; but if we fcan
Gods word aright, his works far fhort doe fall :
The word is God, the works are creatures all.
The fundry peeces of this generall frame
Are dimmer letters, all which fpell the fame
Eternall word. But thefe cannot expreffe
His greatneffe with fuch eafie readineffe,
And therefore yeeld. For heaven fhall pafs away,
The Sun, the Moon, the Stars, fhall all obey
To light one generall bone-fire ; but his word
His builder up, his all deftroying fword
Yet ftill furvives, no jot of that can dye,
Each tittle meafures immortality.

                                        Once

Once more this mighty word his people greets,
Thus lapp'd and thus swath'd up in Paper sheets.
Read here Gods Image with a zealous eye,
The legible and written Deity.

Upon some pieces of work in York House.

VIew this large Gallery faced with mats and
    Is it not purer then *Joves* milky way? (say,
Which should he know, mortals might justly fear
He would forsake his Heaven and sojourne here.

Here on a River rides a silver swan,
Vailing her swelling sailes, and hath began
Her merry will, and left Meander dry,
Rather intending in this place to dye.
So curious is the work, the art so sweet,   (feet.
That men stand back lest they should wet their

Here s *Joseph* and his Brethren, he in state
Enthroned in a Chaire, his dream his fate.
His brethren they stand bare, and though the board
Be dumb, each posture of them call him Lord.
Joseph conceals his tears with hard restraint,
                                            (paint.
Which would gush out should they not spoile the
                                            Under

Under a tree whose arms were wide displayed
And broidered with blossomes, *Venus* layed
Her naked body, which when men espy,
Modesty 'gins to check the saucy eye,
They steal a look ; but why ? lest she, they say;
Seeing them look should rise and run away.
Well doth the Sun refuse his face to shew,
Blushing to see so faire a face below :
Which had *Pigmalion* seen so truely faire,
He would have married streight and sav'd his
For life, which was the others only bliss (prayer.
He beg'd of *Venus*, art ha th given this.

Divert your eye from this seducing sight,
And see the Dear & Heardgrooms harmelesfight,
One gasping lies, where with consenting strife,
The Painter and the poorman tug for life.
Well may you say that see his hanging head,
The Pictures lively, though the man be dead.

Open the door and let my eyes come in,
A place that would entice a Saint to sin ;
Almost too dear for man to tread upon,
A floor all diaperd with Marble stone,
Feet touch our feet. This mystery beguiles
Philosophy of many thousand wiles.
Nay to encrease the miracle ; with ease
We here become our own Antipodes.
What ruder age did think the best of all,
γνῶθι σέαυτ ν hangs on every wall,
Quite hung with it, where every eye may see
Not more what we doe seem then what we be.

D   The

The glaſſe ſo ſteals us from us that you'd ſwear
That we the ſhadow that the ſubſtance were,
Which doth not take impreſſion but doth give.
Here might *Narciſſus* ſee himſelfe and live;
Nor for the pleaſure of one fading houre,
Eternally be damn'd into a flower.

Sir Henry Wotton *on*
Q: *ELIZABETH.*

YE glorious trifles of the Eaſt,
  Whoſe eſtimation fancies raiſe,
  Pearles, Rubies, Saphirs, and the reſt
Of precious Gems, what is your praiſe
When as the Diamond ſhewes his raiſe?

  Ye Violets that firſt appear,
By your blew Purple Matles known,
  Like the proud virgins of the year,
As if the ſpring were all your own,
What are you when the Roſe is blown?

  Ye leſſer beauties of the night,
That weakly ſatisfies our eyes
  More by your number then your light,
Like common people of the skies,
What are ye when the Moon doth riſe?

                                          Ye

Ye warbling chanters of the wood,
That still our eares with natures layes,
   Thinking your paſſions underſtood
By accents weak. What is your praiſe
When *Philomel* her notes doth raiſe ?

   So when my Princeſſe ſhall be ſeen
In ſweetneſſe of her looks and mind,
   By vertue firſt then choiſe a Queen ;
Tell whether ſhe were not aſſing'd
To ecclipſe the glory of her kind.

   The Roſe, the Violet, and the whole ſpring
May to her breath for ſweetneſſe run,
   The Diamonds darkned in the ring ;
When ſhe appears the Moons undone,
As at the brightneſſe of the Sun.

D 2

On

On the Princes birth.

WEll fare the Muses which in well chimb'd
    Our Princes noble birth do sing, (verse
I have a heart as full of joy as theirs,
  As full of duty to my King :
      And thus I tell
      How every bell
    Did sound forth *Englands* merry glee ;
      The boon-fires too
      With much adoe,
  It were great pitty to belye her,
  Made *London* seem as all one fire ;
    A joyfull sight to see.

The wisest Citizens were drunk that day,
  With Bear and wine most soundly paid :
The Constables in duty reeld away,
  And charged others them to aide.
      To see how soon
      Both Sun and Moon
    And seven Stars forgotten be :
      But all the night
      Their heads were light

                         With

With much exalting of their horne,
Because the Prince of *Wales* was borne;
　　A joyfull sight to see.

The Dutchmen they were drunk six dayes before
　And prayed us to excuse their joy.
The Frenchmen vow'd nere to be sober more,
　But drink healths to the royall boy
　　　In their own wine
　　　Both brisk and fine.
　　The valient Irish cram a cree,
　　　It pledged hath
　　　In Usquebath :
　And being in a joviall vaine
They made a bog even of their braine :
　　A joyfull sight to see.

The *Scots* in bonny Ale their joy did sing,
　And wisht this royall babe a man,
That they might beg him for to be their King,
　And let him rule them when he can,
　　　The *Spaniards* made
　　　A shrug and said,
　　After my pipe come follow me ;
　　　Canary Sack
　　　Did go to rack,
Our Gentlemen with them took part,
The Papists drunk it with an heart :
　　A joyfull sight to see.

　　　D 3　　　　　　　　A

A *Welch* for joy her owen Prince was born,
    Doe mean to change St. *Davids* day,
Swearing no leeks hereafter shall be worne
    But on the twenty ninth of *May.*
        None so merry
        Drinking Perry
    And Metheglin on her knee,
        Every man
        His crock and can :
Thus arm'd the Devill they defied,
And durst tell *Belzebub* she lyed :
    A joyfull sight to see.

But whilst the bells about us made a din,
    And boon-fires for our Prince we make ;
The Puritans doe onely burne within
    Spirituall fagots for his sake,
        Should they maintaine
        A fire prophane
    They'd rather martyrs wish to be .
        But this remit
        Till Judges sit,
Next Sessions some or other may
Find wholesome Tyburne in their way :
    A joyfull sight to see.

                        A Letter

A Letter to his Miſtreſſe.

GO happy Paper, by command
  Take liberty to kiſſe an hand
More white then any part of thee,
Although with ſpots thou graced be.
The glory of the chiefeſt day,
The morning aire perfum'd in *May* :
The firſt-borne Roſe of all the ſpring,
The down beneath the Turtles wing ;
A Lute juſt reaching to the eare,
What ere is ſoſt is ſweet is faire,
Are but her ſhreds, who fills the place
And ſumme of every ſingle grace.
  As in a child the nurſe diſcries,
The mothers lips, the fathers eyes,
The uncles noſe, and doth apply
Honours to every part ; ſo I
In her could analize the ſtore
Of all the choice ere nature wore ;
Each private peece to minde may call
Some Earth, but none can match it all ;
Poor Emblems they can but expreſſe
One Element of comlineſſe ;

       D 4   None

None are so rich to shew in one
All simples of perfection :
Nor can the Pencil represent
More then the outward lineament ;
Then who can limbe the Portraiture
Of beauties live behaviour :
Or what can figure every kind
Of jewels that adorne the mind ?
Thought cannot draw her Picture full,
Each thought to her is grosse, is dull.

On the *Earle* of Pembroke's Death.

Did not my sorrows sighd into a verse(hearse;
    Deck the sad pomp and mourning of thy
I'd swear thy death the birth of hasty fame,
Begot to try our sorrowes with thy name.
Ile not believe it yet ; it cannot sort
With earnest thou shouldst dye of meere report :
Newes cannot kill, nor is the common breath,
Fate, or infection.   Shalt I think that death
Struck with so rude a hand, so without art
To kill, and use no Preface to his dart.   (eares
Come *Pembroke* lives. Oh doe not fright our
With such destroying truth, first raise our fears
                   And

And say he is not well ; that will suffice
To force a river from the publick eyes.
Or if he must be dead, Oh let the newes
 Speak't in a stonish'd whisper, let it use   (cloud
Some phrase without a voyce, 'twould too much
Our apprehension should it speak aloud.
Let's hear it in a Riddle, or so told
As if the labouring sence grieved to unfold
Its doubtfull woe. Hadst thou endured the gout,
Or lingring of thy Doctor (which no doubt
Had bin the worse disease) the publick zeal
Had conquered fate and sav'd thee ; but to steal
A close departure from us, and to dye
Of no disease, but of a Prophesie,
Is mystery not fate : nor wert thou kild
Like other men, but like a type fulfilld.
So suddenly to dye is to deceive ;
Nor was it death, but a not taking leave :
Tis true the shortnesse doth forbid to weep,
For so our Fathers dying fell asleep :
So *Enoch* whilst his God he did adore,
Instead of suffering death was seen no more.
But oh this is too much, and we should wrong
Thy ashes, thought we not this speed to long.
Methinks a dream had serv'd, or silent breath,
Or a still pulse, or something like to death.
Now twere detraction to suppose a tear,
Or the sad weeds which the glad mourners wear
Could value such a losse. He that mourns thee
Must bring an eye can weep an Elegy :

A

A look that would save blacks, whose heavy grace
Chides mirth, and wears a funerall in the face :
Whose fighs are with such feeling sorrow blown
That all the aire he draws returns a groan.
That griefe doth neareſt fit that is begun (done.
When the year ends and when the blacks are

    Thou needſt no guilded Tomb, superfluous coſt
Is beſt beſtowed on them whose names are loſt.
Hadſt thou no Statue, thy great memory
Were Marble to it ſelfe, the bravery
Of Jet or rich Enammel were miſpent
Where the brave Courſe is its own ornament.
In thee ſhine all high parts, which falſly wit
Or flattering raptures for their Lord beget,
When they would faigne an Epitaph, and write
As if their griefe made legs when they indite ;
Such dutifull untruths, that ere he grieve,
The Readers firſt toile is how to believe.
Thy greatneſſe was no Idoll, ſtate in thee
Receiv'd its luſtre from humility.
He that will blame thy Coat, and onely looks
How thou wer't Noble by the Heraulds books,
Miſtakes thy linage; and admiring blood,
Forgets thy beſt deſcent, vertue and good.
Theſe are too great for Scutcheons, and made thee
Without fore-fathers thine own Pedigree.

Upon

Upon his chast Mistresse.

Love, give me leave to serve thee, and be wise;
To keep thy torch in, and restore blind eyes:
Ile such a flame into my bosome take,
As Martyrs court when they embrace the stake :
No dull and smoaky fire, but heat divine,
That burns not to consume but to refine.
   I have a Mistresse for perfections rare
In every eye, but in my thoughts most faire.
Like tapers on the Altar shine her eyes,
Her breath is the perfume of sacrifice :
And wheresoever my fancy would begin,
Still her perfection lets Religion in.
I touch her as my beads without devout care,
And come unto my courtship as my prayer.
We sit and talk and kisse away the houres
As chastly, as the mornings dew kisse flowers.
We were no flesh, but one another greet
As blessed soules in seperation meet.
I might have lustfull thoughts to her of all
Earths heavenly quire the most Angelicall ,
But looking in my brest her forme I find
That like my Guardian Angell keeps my mind
                               From

From rude attempts, and when affections ftir
I calme all paffions with one thought of her.
Thus they whofe reafon loves, and not their fence,
The fpirit love. Thus on intelligence
Reflects upon his like, and by chaft loves
In the fame fphear this and that Angel moves :
Nor is this barren love : each noble thought
Begets another, and that ftill is brought
To bed of more, vertues and grace encreafe ;
And fuch a numerous iffue nere can ceafe :
Where children (though great bleffings) onely be
Pleafures repriev'd to fome poftery.
Beafts love like men, if men in luft delight,
And call that love which is but appetite.
When Effence meets with Effence, and fouls joyn
In mutuall knots, thats the true nuptiall twine.
    Such Lady is my love, and fuch is true ;
    All other love is to your fex, not you.

On

On a Painters handsome Daughter.

SUch are your Fathers Pictures, that we doe
Believe they are not counterfeit but true :
So lively and so fresh that we may swear
Instead of draughts he hath placed creaturesthere,
People not shadowes ; which in time will be
Not a dead number but a colony.
Nay more; yet some think they have skill and arts,
That they are well bred, pictures of good parts ;
And you your selfe faire *Julia* doe disclose
Such beauties that you may seem one of those,
That having motion gaind at least and sence,
Began to know it selfe and stole from thence ;
Whilst thus his æmulous art with nature strives,
Some think h'hath none, others he hathtwo wives.
If you love none (faire maide) but look on all,
You then among his set of Pictures fal! ;
If that you look on all and love all men,
The Pictures too will be your Sisters then.
Your choise must shew you are of another fleece,
And tell you are his daughter not his piece.

All

All other proofes are vaine, go not about; (doubt.
We two will embrace, and love, and clear the
(will know
When you have brought forth your like the world
You are his Child ; what Picture can doe so ?

To Dr. Price writing Anni-
verfaries on
Prince HENRY.

Even fo dead *Hector* thrice was triumph'd on (done
The walls of *Troy*, thrice flaine when fate had
So did the barbarous *Greeks* before their houſt
Turmoile his aſhes and prophane his Ghoſt :
As *Henryes* vault, his pure and ſacred hearfe
Is torne and batter'd by thy Anniverfe.
Waſt not enough nature and ſtrength were foes,
Unleſſe thou yearly murther him in profe.
Or didſt thou hope thy ravening verfe could make
A louder eccho then the Almanack.
Truſt me *November* doth more gaſtly look
In *Dades* and *Hopſons* penniworth then thy book;
And ſadder record their fixt figure bears,
Then thy falfe Printed and ambitious tears.

                                                    And

And wer't not for Chriſtmas which is nigh,
When fruits, when eaten and digeſted Pye
Call for more paper, no man could make ſhift
How to employ thy writing to his thriſt.
Wherefore forbear for pitty or for ſhame,
And let ſome richer pen redeem his name
From rottenneſſe ; then leave him captive, ſince
So vile a price nere ranſom'd ſuch a Prince.

A Reply upon an Anſwer to the former Copy.

NOr is it grieved, grave you the memory
Of ſuch a ſtory, ſuch a book as he, (read :
That ſuch a Copy might through the world be
Yet *Henry* lives though he be buried.
It could be wiſhd that every day would bear
Him one good witneſſe that he ſtill were here.
That ſorrow rul'd the year, and by this Sun
Each man could tell thee how the day had run.
O 't were an honeſt cauſe for him could ſay,
I have bin buſie and wept out the day
Remembring him. His name would ever laſt,
Were ſuch a trophy, ſuch a banner plac'd
Upon his grave as this ; Here a man lies
Was kild by *Henryes* dart not deſtinies.

But

But for a Cobler to throw up his cap
And cry the Prince the Prince; O dire mishap!
Or a *Geneva* bridegroom after Grace
To throw his spouse ith' fire, or scratch her face
To the tune of the lamentation, and delay
His friday capon to the Sabbath day;
Or an old Popish Lady halfe vowed dead
To fast away the day in gingerbread;
For him to write such Annals : all these things
Doe open laughter and shut up griefes springs.
Wherefore *Vertumnus* if youle Print the next,
Bring better notes, or chuse a fitter text.

On a Lady that dyed of the small pox.

O Thou deformed unwomanlike desease!
    That plowest up flesh and blood and sowest
                                (there peace;
And leav'st such prints on beauty if thou come,
As clouted shoon doe in a floare of loame :
Thou that of faces honicombs dost make,
And of two breasts two cullinders ; forsake
Thy deadly trade, thou now art rich, give ore
And let our curses call thee forth no more,
Or if thou needs wilt magnifie thy power
Goe where thou art invoked every hour
                                Amongst

Amongst the gamesters, where they name thee
At the last man or the last pocky nick.   (thick
Thou who hast such superfluous store of gaine,
Why strikst thou one whose ruine is thy shame ?
                                                                                (kist,
O thou hast murdred where thou shouldst have
And where thy shaft was needful, there thou mist.
Thou shouldst have chosen out some homely face
Where thy ill-favourd kindnes might add grace,
That men might say, how beautious once was she,
And what a curious piece was mard by thee :
Thou shouldst have wrought on some such Lady-
That never loved her Lord nor ever could (mould
Untill she were deformed ; thy tyranny
Were then within the rules of charity.
But upon one whose beauty was above
All sorts of art, whose love was more then love.
On her to fix thy ugly counterfeit,
Was to erect a Piramid of jet,
And put out fire ; to dig a turfe from Hell,
And place it where a gentle soule should dwell
A soule which in the body would not stay,
When twas no more a body, nor pure clay,
But a huge ulcer ; ô thou heavenly race,
Thou soule that shunst the infection of thy case,
Thy house, thy prison, pure soule, spotless faire,
Rest where no heat, no cold, no compounds are.
Rest in that country, and enjoy that ease,
Which thy fraile flesh denied, and thy disease.

Upon the *Kings Returne* to the City
of London *when he came last thether from*
Scotland *and was entertained there*
by the Lord Mayor.

SIng and be merry King *Charles* is come back,
Lets drink round his health with Claret & Sack:
The *Scots* are all quiet, each man with his pack
May cry now securely, come see what you lack.
   Sing and be merry boyes, sing and be merry,
   London's a fine Town so is *London-Derry.*

Great preparation in *London* is made
To bid the King welcome each man gives his aide,
With thankfgiving cloths themselves they arrayd
(I should have said holy-day) but I was afraid.
   Sing *&c.*

They stood in a row for a congratulation
Like a company of wild-geese in the old fashion :
Railes in the Church are abomination,
But Railes in the street are no innovation.
   Sing *&c.*

My

My Lord Mayor himselfe on cock-horse did ride
Not like a youngGallant with a sword by his side
Twas carried before him, but there was espied
The crosse-bar in the hilt by a Puritan eyed.
   Sing &c.

Two dozen of Aldermen ride two by two, (blew:
Their Gowns were all scarlet, but their noses were
The Recorder made a speech, if report it be true,
He promis'd more for them then ere they will do.
   Sing &c.
                    (the State,
They should be good subjects to the King and
The Church they would love, no Prelates would
But methinks it was an ominous fate   (hate;
They brought not the King thorow Bishops-gate.
   Sing &c.

The Citizens rod in their Golden Chaines
Fetch'd from St. *Martyns,* no region of *Spaines* :
It seems they were trobl'd with *Gundamors* pains,
Some held by their pummels and some by their
   Sing &c.   (manes.

In Jackets of Velvet, without Gown or Cloak,
Their faces were wainscot, their harts were ofoke:
No Trainbands were seen, no drums beat a stroke,
Because City Captains of late have been broke.
   Sing &c.

The King Queen and Prince, the Palsgrave of
With two branches more of the royal vine(*Rhine*
Rod to the *Guild-Hall* where they were to dine,
There could be no lack where the Conduits run
    Sing &c.   (wine.

Nine hundred dishes in the bill of fare
For the King and Nobles prepared there were ;
There could be no lesse a man might well swear
By the widgeons and woodcocks and geese that
    Sing &c.   (were there.

Though the dinner were long yet the grace was
                                 (but short,
It was said in the fashion of the English Court.
But one passage more I have to report,
Small thanks for my paines I look to have fort.
    Sing &c.

Down went my Lord Mayor as low as his knee,
Then up went the white of an Aldermans eye :
We thought the Bishops grace enlarged should be
(Not the Arch-Bishops)no such meaning had he.
    Sing &c.

When's Lordship kneeld down we lookd he should
(So he did heartily but in his own way)   (pray,
The cup was his book, the collect for the day
Was a health to King *Charles*, all out he did say.
    Sing &c.

                                  The

The forme of prayer my Lord did begin
The reſt of the Aldermen quickly were in :
One *Warner* they had of the greatneſſe of the ſin
Without diſpenſation from *Burton* or *Prin.*
    Sing *&c.*

Before they had done it grew towards night,
(I forget my Lord Mayor was made a Knight :
The Recorder too with another wight,
Whom I cannot relate, for the torches are light.
    Sing *&c.*

Up and away by St. *Pauls* they paſſe ;
When a prickear d brayd like a Puritan aſs (glaſſe
Some thought he had been ſcar'd with the painted
He ſwore not but cry'd high Popery by th' maſſe.
    Sing *&c.*

The Quire with Muſick on a Scaffold they ſee
In Surplices all their Tapers burnt by,
An Anthem they ſung moſt melodiouſly ,
If this were Popery I confeſſe it was high.
    Sing *&c.*

From thence to *WhiteHall* there was made no ſtay
Where the King gave them thanks for their love
Nothing was wanting if I could but ſay (that day,
The Houſe of Commons had met him half way.
    Sing *&c.*

Upon the Kings-Book bound up
in a Cover coloured with
His Blood.

LEt abler pens commend thofe leaves ; whofe
  fame
Spreads through all languages, through time
    whofe name ;
Nor can thofe Tongues add glory to this book
So great, as they from the tranflation took.
Shine then rare piece in thine own *Charls* his ray ;
Yet fuffer me thy covering to difplay,
And tell the world that this plain fanguine vail
A beauty far more glorious doth conceal
Then masks of Ladies : and although thou be
A Book, where every leafe's a Library
Fil'd with choife Gems of th' Arts, Law, Gofpel ;
The chiefeft Jewel is the Cabinet.   (yet
A fhrine much holier then the Saint ; you may
To this as harmeleffe adoration pay,
As thofe that kneel to Martyrs tombs, for know,
This facred blood doth *Rome* a Relique fhow
Richer then all her fhrines, and then all thofe
More hallowed far, far more miraculous. (none
Thus cloth'd go forth, bleff'd Book, and yield to
But to the Gofpel, and Chrifts blood alone.
                                        Thy

Thy Garments now like his ; so juſt the ſame,
As he from *Bozra*, and the wine-preſſe came ;
Both purpled with like gore : where you may ſee
This on the Scaffold, that upon the Tree
Pour'd out to ſave whole Nations. O may't lye
Speechleſſe like that, and never never cry
Vengence, but pray father forgive theſe too,
(Poor ignorant men !) they know not what they
(doe.

Upon the Nuptials of John
Talbot *Eſquire, and* Miſtreſſe
Elizabeth Kite.

COme grand *Apollo* tune my Lyre
To harmonize in th' Muſes Quire,
  Give me a draught of Helicon,
Let *Pindus* and *Parnaſſus* prove
Propitious in the ſlights of love,
  Though diſtanc'd now at *Eberton.*

A conſecrated quill I know,
Pluck'd from the ſilver'd Swan of Po,
  Love-tales is onely fit to write,
But ſince tis voted by the Stoick,
Not place nor pen doth make the Poet,
  Ile venture with a plume of th' Kite.

Not

Not for to blazen the great name
Of th' *Talbots* never dying fame
   Eterniz'd in all Histories,
Ile onely say the *Trojan* wit,
Which *Helen* stole, must now submit
   To *Talbot* in loves mysteries.

For neither *Egypt*, *Troy*, nor *Greece*,
Nor *Colchis* with her Golden-Fleece
   Hath ever ought produc'd so rare
In vertue, beauty, every Grace
That dignifies the mind or face,
   Which with this Couple may compare.

The holy Priest hath firmely tied
The Gordian knot, that twill abide
   The touch of what's Canonicall ;
And th' Pigmie Justice hath fast chain'd
The Bugbeare Act, though it be proclaim'd
   As simple, as Apocryphall

Let's hasten therefore them to bring
To th' pleasant fountaine whence doth spring
   The joyes of *Cupids* Monarchy ;
There tumbling on their Nuptiall bed
To batter for a Maiden-head,
   Twind like the Zodiack Geminie.

Hence dull ey'd *Somnus* think not now
T'inthrone upon this Ladies brow,

                 Far

Far choycer joyes doe her invite :
For she's now anchor'd in a Haven
Where sacred *Hymen* her hath given
   An other Soveraigne of the night.

Come draw the curtains, lets depart,
And leave two bodies in one heart
   Devoted to a restlesse rest.
And when their virgin Lamps expire,
May there arise from the same fire
   An other *Phœnix* in the Nest.

Upon Aglaura *Printed in Folio.*

BY this large margent did the Poet mean
  To have a Comment wrote upon the Scene ?
Or else that Ladies, who doe never look
But in a Poem or in a Play-book,
May in each page have space to scrible down
When such a Lord or fashion came to Town ;
As Swains in Almanacks their counts doe keep
                       (their sheep.
When their cow calv'd and when they bought
Ink is the life of Paper, 'tis meet then
That this which scap'd the Presse should feel the
A room with one side furnish'd, or a face (pen,
Painted halfe way, is but a foule disgrace.
                    This

This great voluminous Pamphlet may be said
To be like one who hath more haire then head :
More excrement then body, trees which sprout
With breadest leaves have still the smallest fruit.
When I saw so much white I did begin
To think *Aglaura* either did lye in,
Or else did pennance : never did I see
Unlesse in Bills dash'd in the *Chancery*
So little in so much, as if the feet
Of Poetry were sold like Law by the sheet.
Should this new fashion last but one halfe year,
Poets as Clarks would make our Paper deare.
Doth not that Artist erre and blast his fame
That sets out Pictures lesser then the frame :
Was ever Chamberlain so mad to dare
To lodge a Child in the great Bed of *Ware*.
Aglaura would please better did she lye
Ith' narrow bounds of an Epitome.
Those pieces that are wove of th' finest twist,
As Velvet, Plush, have still the smallest list.
She that in *Persian* habits made such brags
Degenerates in the excesse of rags :
Who by her Giant bulk this onely gaines
Perchance in Libraries to hang in chaines.
Tis not in books as cloth, we never say
Make *London* measure when we buy a Play,
But rather have them par'd ; those leaves are
To the judicious which most spotted are.   (faire
Give me the sociable pocket books,
These empty Folio's onely please the Cooks.

                                        Venus

Venus lachrimans.

WAke my *Adonis* doe not dye,
    One life's enough for thee and I ;
    Where are thy words, thy wiles,
    Thy love, thy frowns, thy smiles ;
    Alasse in vaine I call,
    One death hath snatch'd them all :
Yet death's not deadly in thy face,
Death in those looks it selfe hath grace.
    Twas this, twas this I feard
    When thy pale ghost appeard :
This I presag'd when thundering *Jove*
Tore the best myrtle in my Grove ;
When my sick rosebuds lost their smell,
And from my Temples untouch'd fell ;
    And twas for some such thing
    My Dove did hang her wing.
Whether art thou my Diety gone,
Venus in *Venus* there is none :
In vaine a Goddesse now am I
Onely to grieve and not to dye.
    But I will love my griefe,
    Make tears my tears reliefe :

              And

And sorrows shall to me
A new *Adonis* be ;
And this no fates can rob me of, whiles I
A goddesse am to weep but not to dye.

An Ode in the praise of Sack.

1.

HEar me as if thy eares had palate Jack,
I sing the praise of Sack :
Hence with *Apollo* and the muses nine,
Give me a cup of wine.
Sack will the soule of Poetry infuse,
Be that my theam and muse.
But *Bacchus* I adore no Diety,
Nor *Bacchus* neither unlesse Sack he be.

2.

Let us by reverend degrees draw nere,
I feel the Goddesse here.
Loe I, dread Sack, an humble Priest of thine
First kisse this cup thy shrine,
That with more hallowed lips and inlarg'd soule
I may receive the whole :
Till *Sibill*-like full with my God I lye,
And every word I speak be Prophesie.

Come

3.

Come to this Altar you that are opprest,
    Or otherwise distrest,
Here's that will further grivances prevent,
    Without a Parliament :
With fire from hence if once your blood be warm
    Nothing can doe you harme ;   (feel
When thou art arm'd with Sack, thou canst not
Though thunder strike thee ; that hath made thee
                        (steel.

4.

Art sick man ? doe not bid for thy escape
    A cock to *Aesculape* ;
If thou wouldst prosper, to this Altar bring
    Thy gratefull offring,
Touch but the shrine, that does the God enclose,
    And streight thy feaver goes
Whilst thou immaginst this, hee's given thee
Not onely heath but immortality.

5.

Though thou wert dumb as is the scaly fry
    In *Neptunes* royalty :
Drink but as they doe, and new wayes shalt find
    To utter thy whole mind ;
When Sack more severall language has infus'd
    Then *Babels* builders used :
                     And

And whensoever thou thy voyce shalt raise,
No man shall understand but all shall praise.

6.

Hath cruell nature so thy senses bound
    Thou canst not judge of sounds ?
Loe where yon narrow fountaine scatters forth
    Streams of an unknown worth :
The heavenly musick of that murmure there
    Would make thee turne all eare ;
And keeping time with the harmonious flood,
Twixt every bubble thou shalt cry good good.

7.

Has fortune made thee poor, dost thou desire
    To heap up glorious mire ?
Come to this stream where every drop's a Pearl
    Might buy an Earl :
Drench thy selfe soundly here and thou shalt rise
    Richer then both the Indies.
So mayest thou still enjoy with full content
Midas his wish without his punishment.

8.

All this can Sack, and more then this Sack can,
    Give me a fickle man   (what,
That would be somewhat faine but knows not
    There is a cure for that :

                       Let

Let him quaffe freely of this powerfull flood,
    He shall be what he would.
To all our wishes Sack content does bring,
And but our selves can make us every thing.

An Epitaph on some bottles of Sack and Claret laid in sand.

ENter and see this tomb (Sirs) doe not fear
No spirits but of Sack will fright you here :
Weep ore this tomb, your waters here may have
Wine for their sweet companion in this grave.
A dozen *Shakespears* here inter'd doe lye ;
Two dozen *Johnsons* full of Poetry.
Unhapry Grapes could not one pressing doe,
But now at last you must be buried too :
Twere commendable sacriledge no doubt
Could I come at your graves to steal you out.
Sleep on but scorne to dye, immortall liquor,
The burying of thee thus shall make thee quicker.
Mean while thy friends pray loud that thou maist
A speedy resurrection from thy grave.   (have

How

How to choose a Mistresse.

HEr for a Mistresse would I faine enjoy
That hangs out lip and pouts at every toy ;
Speaks like a wag, is bold, dares stoutly stand
And bids love welcome with a wanton hand :
If she be modest wise and chast of life,
Hang her she's good for nothing but a wife.

Upon a Picture.

BEhold those faire eyes, in whose sight
Sparkles a lustre no lesse bright
Then that of rising Stars when they
Would make the night outshine the day.
To those pure lips the humming be,
May as to blooming Roses flee :
The wanton wind about doth hurle,
Courting in vaine that lovely curle ;
And makes a murmure in despaire,
To dally the unmooved haire.
View but the cheeks where the red Rose
And Lilly white a beauty growes,

So

So orient as might adorne
The flowing of the brightest morne.
Sure 'tis no Picture, nere was made
So much perfection in a shade :
Her shape is soule enough to give
A sencelesse Marble power to live.
If this an Idoll be, no eye
Can ever scape Idolatry.

On Ladies Attire.

YOn Ladies that wear Cypresse vailes,
   Turn'd lately to white linnen rayles ;
And to your girdles wear your bands,
And shew your armes instead of hands.
What could you doe in Lent so meet
As, fittest dresse, to wear a sheet ?
Twas once a band, tis now a cloak ;
A acorne one day proves a oak.
Weare but your linnens to your feet
And then the band will be a sheet.
By which device and wise excesse
You doe your pennance in a dresse :
And none shall know by what they see
Which Ladies censur'd, and which free.

F   *The*

The Answer.

Black Cypresse vailes are shrowds of night,
White linnen railes are rayes of light,
Which to our girdles though we wear
We have armes to keep your hands off there.
Who makes our hands to be our cloak,
Makes John a stiles of John a noak.
We wear our linnen to our feet,
Yet need not make our band our sheet
Your Clergy wear as long as we,
Yet that implies conformity.
Be wise, recant what you have writ,
Least you doe pennance for your wit;
And least loves charmes doe weave a string
To tye you as you did your Ring.

On

On a Gentlewoman that had the Small-Pox.

A Beauty smoother then the Ivory plaine,
Late by the Pox injuriously was slaine.
Twas not the Pox, love shot a thousand darts
And made those pits for graves to bury hearts :
But since that beauty hath regaind its light,
Those hearts are doubly slaine it shines so bright.

On a faire Gentlewomans blistered lip.

H Ide not your sprouting lip, nor kill
The juicie bloom with bashfull skill :
Know it is an amorous dew
That swells to court your corall hew.
And what a blemish you esteem
To other eyes a Pearl may seem ;
Whose watry growth is not above
The thrifty seine which Pearls doe love :

F 2   And

And doth so well become that part
That chance may seem a secret art :
Doth any judge the face lesse faire
Whose tender silk a moal doth bear ?
Are apples thought lesse sound and sweet
When honey specks and red doe meet ?
Or will a Diamond shine lesse clear
If in the midst a soile appear ?
Then is your lip made fairer by
Such sweetnesse of deformity.
The Nectar which men strive to sip
Springs like a well upon your lip.
Nor doth it shew immodesty,
But overflowing chastity.
O who will blame the fruitfull trees
When too much gum or sap he sees ?
Here nature from her store doth send
Onely what other parts can lend.
If lovely buds ascend so high,
The root below cannot be dry.

To his Mistresse.

KEepe on your mask and hide your eye,
For in beholding you I dye.
Your fatall beauty Gorgon-like
Dead with astonishment doth strike.

　　　　　　　　　　　Your

Your piercing eyes that now I see
Are worse then Basilisks to me.
Shut from mine eyes those hills of snow,
Their melting vally doe not shew :
Those azure pathes lead to dispaire,
Oh vex me not, forbear, forbear ;
For while I thus in torments dwell,
The sight of Heaven is worse then Hell.
In those faire cheeks two pits doe lye
To bury those slaine by your eye :
So this at length doth comfort me,
That fairely buried I shall be :
My grave with Roses, Lillies, spread,
Methinks tis life for to be dead :
Come then and kill me with your eye,
For if you let me live, I dye.

     When I perceive your lips againe
Recover those your eyes have slaine,
With kisses that (like bilsome pure)
Deep wounds as soon as made doe cure ;
Methinks tis sicknesse to be sound,
And theres no health to such a wound.
When in your bosome I behold
Two hills of snow yet never cold :
Which lovers, whom your beauty kills,
Revive by climing those your hills.
Methinks theres life in such a death
That gives a hope of sweeter breath.
Then since one death prevailes not where
So many Antidotes are nere :

           F 3   And

And your bright eyes doe but in vaine
Kill those who live as fast as flaine ;
That I no more fuch death furvive,
Your way's to bury me alive
In place unknown, and fo that I
Being dead may live and living dye.

A lover to one difpraifing his Miſtreſſe.

WHy flight you her whom I approve :
    Thou art no peere to try my love ;
Nor canſt diſcerne where her forme lies,
Unleſſe thou faweſt her with my eyes.
Say ſhe were foule, or blacker then
The night, or Sun-burnt *African* ;
If lik't by me, 'tis I alone
Can make a beauty where there's none :
For rated in my fancy ſhe
Is fo as ſhe appears to me.
Tis not the feature of a face
That doth my faire Election grace.
Nor is my fancy onely led
By a well temper'd white and red ;
Could I enamour'd grow on thoſe,
The Lilly and the bluſhing Roſe

                            United

United in one ftalk might be
As dear unto my thoughts as fhe,
But I look farther and doe find
A richer beauty in her mind :
Where fomething is fo lafting faire,
As time and age cannot impaire.
Hadft thou a profpective fo cleare
That thou couldft view my object there ;
When thou her vertues didft efpy,
Thoudft wonder and confeffe that I
Had caufe to like ; and learne from hence
To love by judgement, not by fence.

On the death of a faire Gentle-
womans Robin-redbreft.

WHatfoere birds in groves are bred
Provide your anthems, *Robins* dead.
Poor *Robin* that was wont to neft
In faire *Siloras* lovely breft,
And thence would peep into her eye,
To fee what feather ftood awry.
This pretty bird might freely fip
The fugered Nectar from her lip.
When many love-burnt foules have pined
To fee their rivall fo retained.

But

But what caufed *Robins* death was this,
Robin fur.. furfeited with bliffe ;
Or elfe canfe her faire cheek poffeft
A purer red then *Robins* breft,
Wherein confifted all his pride,
The little bird for envy dyed.

On the death of Sir
Tho: Pelham.

Meerely for death to grieve and mourne
Were to repine that man was borne.
When weak old age doth fall afleep
'Twere foul ingratitude to weep.
Those threds alone fhould force out tears
Whofe fuddain crack breaks off fome years.
Here 'tis not fo, full diftance here
Sunders the cradle from the beere.
A fellow-traveller he hath bin
So long with time, fo worn to'th skin,
That were it not juft now bereft
His body firft the foule had left.
Threefcore and ten is natures date,
Our journey when we come in late :
Beyond that time the overplus
Was granted not to him, but us.

For

For his own fake the Sun ne're ftood,
But onely for the peoples good :
Even fo he was held out by aire
Which poor men uttered in their prayer :
And as his goods were lent to give,
So were his dayes that they might live.
So ten years more to him were told
Enough to make another old :
Oh that death would ftill doe fo,
Or elfe on goodmen would beftow
That waft of years which unthrifts fling
Away by their diftempering.
That fome might thrive by this decay
As well as that of land and clay.
Twas now well done : no caufe to mourne
On fuch a feafonable ftone ;
Where death is but a gueft, we finne
Not bidding welcome to his Inne.

    Sleep, fleep, goodman, thy reft embrace,
    Sleep, fleep, th'aft trod a weary race.

Of

Of Musick.

WHen whispering straines with creeping wind
   Distill soft passion through the heart,
And whilst at every touch we find
Our pulses beat and bear a part.
    When threds can make
    Our heart-strings shake ;
    Philosophy can scarce deny
    Our soules consists in harmony.

When unto heavenly joyes we feigne
What ere the soule affecteth most,
Which onely thus we can explaine
By Musick of the winged host :
    Whose rayes we think
    Make stars to wink ;
    Philosophy can scarce deny
    Our soules consist of harmony.

O lul me, lul me, charming aire,
My senses each with wonder sweet ;
Like snow on wool thy fallings are,
Soft like spirits are thy feet.

                    Griefe

Griefe who needs feare
That hath an eare?
Down let him lie
And slumbring dye,
And change his soule for harmony.

To his Mistresse.

ILe tell you how the Rose did first grow red,
And whence the Lillies whitenesse borrowed:
You blusht and streight the Rose with red was
(dight,
The Lillies kiss'd your hands and so grew white.
You have the native colour, these rhe die,
And onely flourish in your livery :
Before that time each Rose was but one staine,
The lilly nought but palenesse did containe.

On a black Gentlewoman.

IF shadowes be a Pictures excellence
And make it seem more glorious to the sence :
If stars in brightest day are lost for sight
And seem more glorious in the mask of night.

Why

Why should you think fair creature that you lack
Perfection cause your eyes and haire are black.
Or that your beauty, which so far exceeds
The new-sprung Lillies in their maidenheads,
The rosie colour of your cheeks and lips
Should by that darknesse suffer an ecclipse.
Rich Diamonds are fairer being set
And compassed within a foile of jet.
Nor can it be dame nature should have made
So bright a Sun to shine without a shade.
It seems that nature when she first did fancy
Your rare composure studied Negromancy :
And when to you these guifts she did impart
She used altogether the Black Art.
She framed the Magick circle of your eyes,
And made those hairs the chains wherein she ties
Rebellious hearts, those vaines, which doe appear
Twined in Meanders about every sphear,
Mysterious figures are, and when you list
Your voyce commandeth like an exorcist.
Now if in Magick you have skill so far
Vouchsafe to make me your familiar.
Nor hath kind nature her black art reveald
By outward parts alone, some are conceald.
As by the spring head men may easily know
The nature of the streams that run below.
So your black eyes and haire doe give direction,
That all the rest are of the like complexion.
The rest where all rest lies that blesseth man,
That *Indian* mine, that streight of Magellan.

                                              The

The worlds dividing gulph, through which who
         (venters
With hoiſed ſailes and raviſhd ſences enters
To a new world of bliſſe. Pardon I pray
If my rude muſe preſumes for to diſplay
Secrets forbid, or hath her bounds ſurpaſt
In praiſing ſweetneſſe which ſhe nere did taſt :
Starv'd men may talk of meat, and blind men may
(Though hid from light) yet know there is a day.
A rover in the mark his arrow ſticks
Sometimes as well as he that ſhoots at pricks.
And if I might direct my ſhaft aright,
The black mark would I hit, and not the white.

- - - - - - - - - - - - - - - - - - - -

On a *Gentlewoman walking*
in the Snow.

I Saw ſaire *Cloris* walk alone,
 When feathered raine came ſoftly downe,
And *Jove* deſcended from his Tower
To court her in a ſilver ſhowre :
The wanton ſnow flew to her breaſt
Like little birds into their neſt,
And overcome with whiteneſſe there
For griefe diſſolv'd into a teare,

       Which

Which trickling down her garments hemme
To deck her freezd into a gemme.

Upon one dead in the snow.

Within a fleece of silent waters drown'd.
Before I met with death a grave I found.
That whil'st it held my life from her sweet home
For griese straight froze it selfe into a Tomb.
Onely one Element my fate thought meet
To be my death, grave, tomb, and winding sheet.
Phœbus himselfe my Epitaph had writ;
But blotting many ere he thought one fit,
He wrote untill my tomb and grave were gone,
And 'twas an Epitaph that I had none.;
For every man that pass'd along that way
Without a sculpture read that there I lay.
Here now the second time inclosed I lye
And thus much have the hast of destiny.
Corruption (from which onely one was free,)
Devour'd my grave, but did not seize on me.
My first grave took me from the race of men,
My last shall give me back to life agen.

On a woman dying in travell the child unborne.

Within this grave there is a grave intombd,
Here lies a mother and a child inwombd.
Twas strange that nature so much vigour gave
To one that nere was born, to make a grave.
Yet an injunction stranger nature willd her,
Poor mother, to be tomb to that which kild her:
And not with so much cruelty content,
Buries the child, the grave, and monument.
Where shall we write the Epitaph? whereon?
The child, the grave, the monument is gone:
Or if upon the child we write a staffe,
Where shall we write the tombs own Epitaph?
Onely this way is left, and now we must
As on a table carpeted with dust
Make chisells of our fingers, and engrave
An Epitaph both on the tomb and grave
Within the dust: but when some hours are gone
Will not the Epitaph have need of one?
I know it well: yet grave it therefore deep
That those which know the losse, may truly weep
A

And shed their tears so justly in that place
Which we before did with a finger trace,
That filling up the letters they may lie
As inlaid Christall to posterity.
Where (as in glasse) if any write another
Let him say thus, here lies a haplesse mother
Whom cruel fate hath made to be a tomb,
And kept in travell till the day of doom.

On Man.

ILl busied man why shouldst thou take such care
To lenghthen out thy lives short callendar ;
Each dropping season, and each flower doth cry
Fool as I fade and wither thou must die.
The beating of thy pulse when thou art well
Is but the towling of thy passing bell :
Night is thy hearse, whose sable Canopy
Covers alike deceased day and thee.
And all those weeping dewes which nightly fall
Are but as tears shed for thy funerall.

On

On Fairesord *windows.*

TEll me you anti-Saints why glasse
With you is longer lived then brasse :
And why the Saints have scap'd their falls
Better from windowes then from walls :
Is it because the brethrens fires
Maintaine a glasse-house in *Black-friers?*
Next which the Church stands North and South,
And East and West the Preachers mouth.
Or ist because such painted ware
Resembles something what you are,
So pied, so seeming, so unsound
In doctrine and in manners found,
That out of emblemattick wit
You spare your selves in sparing it ?
If it be so then *Fairesord* boast,
Thy Church hath kept what all have lost ;
And is preserved from the bane
Of either war or Puritan.
Whose life is colour'd in the paint,
The inside drosse, the outside Saint.

G

On

On a Gentlewoman playing
on the Lute.

BE silent you still musick of the sphears,
And every sence make haste to be all eares ;
And give devout attention to her aires,
To which the Gods doe listen as to prayers
Of pious votaries : the which to hear
Tumult would be attentive, and would swear
To keep lesse noise at *Nile* if there she sing,
Or with a sacred touch grace but one string.
Amongst so many auditors, so many throngs
Of Gods and men, that presse to hear her songs,
Oh let me have an unespied room,
And die with such an anthem ore my tomb.

On Love.

WHen I do love I would not wish to speed,
To plead fruition rather then desire,
But on sweet lingring expectation feed,
And gently would protract not feed my tire.

What

What though my love a martyrdome you
No Salamander ever feels the flame. (name,

That which is obvious I as much esteem
As Courtiors doe old cloths : for novelty
  Doth rellish pleasures, and in them we deem
The hope is sweeter then the memory.
    Injoying breeds a glut, men better tast
    Comforts to come, then pleasures that are
                                        (past.

The Catholick.

I Hold as faith	What *Englands* Church alow
What *Romes* Ch: faith	My conscience disallowes
Where the King is head	That Church can have no shame
The flocks misled	That holds the Pope supreame
Where the Altars drest	There's service scarce divine
The peoples blest	With table bread and wine
He's but an asse	Who the Communion flies
Who shuns the Masse	Is Catholick and wise.

G 2   On

On Faireford *windowes.*

I Know no paint of Poetry
Can mend such colours Imagery
In sullen inke ; Yet *Faireford* I
May rellish thy faire memory.
Such is the ecchoes fainter found ;
Such is the light when Sun is drownd.
So did the fancy look upon
The work before it was begun.
Yet when those shews are out of sight
My weaker colours may delight.
Those Images so faithfully
Report the feature to the eye,
As you would think each picture was
Some visage in a looking-glasse ;
Not a glasse-window face, unlesse
Such as *Cheap-side* hath, when a presse
Of painted Gallants looking out
Bedeck the casement round about.
But these have holy phisnomy ;
Each pane instructs the laity
With silent eloquence, for here
Devotion leads the eye not eare

To

To note the cetechising paint;
Whose easie phrase did so acquaint
Our sence with Gospel that the Creed
In such a hand the weak may read.
Such types can yet of vertue be,
And Christ as in a glasse we see.
Behold two Turtles in one Cage
With such a lovely equipage,
As they who mark them well may doubt
Some young ones have been there stolne out.
When with a fishing rod the Clark
St. *Peters* draught of fish doth mark :
Such is the scale, the eye, the fin,
You'd think they strove and leap'd within :
But if the net which holds them brake
He with his angle some would take.
But would you walk a turne in *Pauls*,
Look up, one little pane inroules
A fairer Temple, fling a stone
The Church is out of the window flown.
Consider but not ask your eyes,
And ghosts at mid-day seem to rise.
The Saints their striving to descend
Are past the glasse and downward bend.
Look there the Devils all would cry,
Did they not see that Christ was by.
See where he suffers for thee, see
His body taken from the tree :
Had ever death such life before?
The limber corps besulkied ore

With

With meager paleneſſe doth diſplay
A middle ſtate 'twixt fleſh and clay :
His armes, his head, his legs, his crown
Like a true Lambskin dangling down :
Who can forbear the grave being nigh
To bring freſh ointment in his eye?
The Puritans were ſure deceiv'd
Who thought thoſe ſhadows mov'd and heav'd.
So held from ſtoning Chriſt ; the wind
And boiſterous tempeſts were ſo kind
As on his Image not to pray,
Whom both the winds and Sea obey.
At *Momus* wiſh be not diſmaied;
For if each Chriſtians heart were glaz'd
With ſuch a window, then each breaſt
Might be his own Evangeliſt.

On the praiſe of an ill-favourd Gentlewoman.

Marry and love thy *Flavia*, for ſhe   (be :
   Hath all things whereby others beautious
For though her eyes be ſmall, her mouth is great,
Though her lips Ivory be, her teeth be jet :
Though they be dark, yet ſhe is light enough,
And though her harſh hair fail, her skin is rough,
                       And

And what if it be yellow, her haires red,
Give her but thine she has a maidenhead.
These things are beauties elements, where these
Compounded are in one she needs must please :
If red and white and each good quality
Be in the wench, nere ask where it doth lye :
In buying things perfumed we ask if there
Be musk and amber in it, but not where.
Though all her parts be not ith' usuall place,
She hath the anagram of a good face.
When by the gam-ut some Musitians make
A perfect song, others will undertake
By the same gam-ut chang'd to equall it :
Things simply good can never be unfit.
For one nights revells silk and gold we use,
But in long journies cloth and leather chuse.
Beauty is barren oft ; and husbands say
There's the best land where is the foulest way.
And what a soveraigne medicine will she be
If thy past sins have taught thee jealousie.
Here needs no spies nor Eunuchs : her commit
Safe to thy foes yea to thy Marmoset.
When *Belgias* Cities th' ruind country drown
That durty foulness armes and guards the Town.
So doth her face guard her, and so for thee,
Which by occasion absent oft mayest be.
She whose face like the clouds turns day to night,
And mightier then the Sea makes Moors seem
                              (white.

Who though sevenyears she in the street hath laid
A Nunnery durst receive and think a maid.
And though in child-bed labour she did lie
Midwives would swear 'twere but a tympany.
If she accuse her selfe, i'le credit lesse
Then witches which impossibles confesse.

Upon Heavens best Image, his faire and vertuous Mistresse
M. S.

THe most insulting tyrant can but be
    Lords of our bodies, still our minds are free.
My Mistres thralls my soul, those chains of Gold
Her locks my very thoughts infetterd hold.
    Then sure she is a Goddesse, and if I
    Should worship her, 'tis no Idolary.

Within her cheeks a fragrant garden lies
Where Roses mixt with Lillies feast mine eyes :
Here's alwayes spring, no winter to annoy
Those heavenly flowers, onely some tears of joy
    Doe water them, and sure if I be wise
    This garden is another Paradice.

(tion
Her eyes two heavenly lamps, whose orderd mo-
Swayes all my reason, my sence, my devotion ;
                    And

And yet those beams did then most glorious shine
When passions dark had maskd this soul of mine ;
   Now if the night her glory best declare,
   What can I deem them but a sta:ry paire.

Her brow is vertues court, where she alone
Triumphant sits in faultlesse beauties throne :
Did you but mark its purenesse, you would swear
'*Diana's* come from Heaven to sojourne there.
   Onely this Cynthia dims not even at noon,
   There wants a man (methinks) in such a Moon.

Her breath is great *Joves* incense, sweeter far
Then all *Arabian* winds and spices are: (twins
Her voyce the sphears best Musick, and those
Her armes a precious paire of Cherubs wings.
   In briefe she is a map of Heaven, and there
   O would that I a constellation were.

The

The black maid to the faire boy.

FAire boy (alaſſe) why flieſt thou me
That languiſh in ſuch flames for thee.
Ime black, tis true ; why ſo is night,
And lovers in dark ſhades delight.
The whole world doe but cloſe your eye
Will be to you as black as I :
Or ope't and view how dark a ſhade
Is by your own faire body made,
Which followes thee where ere thou goe.
O who allowed would not doe ſo :
Then let me ever live ſo nigh,
And thou ſhalt need no ſhade but I.

His Anſwer.

BLack girle complaine not that I fly,
Since fate commands antipathy.
Prodigious muſt that union prove
Where black and white together move :

And

And a conjunction of our lips
Not kisses makes but an ecclipse,
In which the mixed black and white
Pretends more terrour then delight.
Yet if my shadow thou wilt be,
Enjoy thy dearest wish ; but see
Thou keep my shadows property,
And flee away when I come nigh ;
Else stay till death hath blinded me,
And Ile bequeath my selfe to thee.

Verses sent to a Lady, which she
sending back unread, were returned
with this inscription.

REad (faire maid) and know the heat
   That warmes these lines is like the beate.
Thy chast pulse keeps ; thy mornings thought
Hath not more temper.: were there ought
On this virgin paper shed
That might to crimson turne thy red
I should blush for thee , but I vow
Tis all as spotlesse as thy brow.
Read then, and know what art thou hast,
That thus canst make a Poet chast.

The

The Verses.

ON a day ('tis in thy power
To make me blesse or curse that hour)
I saw thy face, thy face then maskd
Like Ivory in Ebon cask'd.
But that dark cloud once drawn away,
Just like the dawning of the day
So brake thy beauty forth, and I
Grew sad, glad, neither, instantly;
Yet through thy mercy, or my chance,
Me thought I saw a pleasing glance
Thou threwst on me : a sugar smile
Dimpled thy cheeks, and all the while
Mirth dancd upon thy brow, to prove
It came from kindnesse if not love.
Oh make it good ; in this let me
Not Poet but a Prophet be.
And think not (fairest) that thy fame
Is wrongd by a Poets Mistresse name ;
Queens have been proud on't, for their Kings
Are but our subjects ; nay all things
Shall unto all posterity
Appear as we will have them, we
Give men valour, maids chastity
And beauty too : if *Homer* would
Hellen had been an hag, and *Troy* had stood.
And though far humbler be my verse,
Yet some there will be will rehearse

And

And like it too perhaps; and then
The life that now thou lendſt my pen
The world ſhall pay thee back agen.

The Nightingale.

MY limbs were weary, and my head oppreſt
With drowſineſſe and yet I could not reſt.
My bed was ſuch no down nor feathers can
Make one more ſoft, though *Jove* again turn Swan
No fear-diſtracted thoughts my ſlumber broke,
I heard no ſcreech-owle ſqueak, nor raven croak;
Nay even the flea (that proud inſulting elfe)
Had taken truce, and was aſleep it ſelfe :   (jewel
But 'twas nights darling, and the woods chiefe
The Nightingale that was ſo ſweetly crewel.
And wooed my ears to rob my eyes of ſleep,
That whilſt ſhe ſung of *Tereus*, they might weep,
And yet rejoyce the tyrant did her wrong,
Her cauſe of woe was burthen of her ſong;
Which whilſt I liſtned too, and greiv'd to hear,
T'was ſuch I could have wiſh'd my ſelfe all eare.
Tis falſe the Poets feigne of *Orpheus*, he
Could neither move a ſtone, a beaſt, nor tree
To follow him; but whereſoere ſhe flies
She makes a grove, where Satyrs and Fairies
About her perch to daunce her roundelayes,
For ſhe ſings ditties to them whilſt *Pan* playes.

Yet

Yet she sung better now, as if in me
She meant with sleep to try the m stery.
But whilst she chanted thus, the Cock for spight
(Dayes hoarser herauld) chid away the night.
Thus rob'd of sleep, mine eyelids nightly guest,
Methought I lay content, though not at rest.

Barclay *his Epitaph.*

HE thats imprisoned in this narrow room
Wer't not for custome needs nor verse nor
Nor can there from these memory be lent (tomb;
To him, who must be his tombs monument ;
And by the vertue of his lasting name
Must make his tomb live long, not it his fame.
For when this gaudy pageantry is gone,
Children of the unborn world shall spy the stone
That covers him, and to their fellowes cry
Just here, just here abouts *Barclay* doth lie.
Let them with faigned titles fortifie
Their tombs, whose sickly vertues fear to die.
And let their tombs belie them, call them blest,
And charitable marble faigns the rest.
He needs not, when lifes true story is done,
The lying proscript of a perjured stone.
Then spare his tomb, thats needlesse and unsafe,
Whose virtue must outlive his Epitaph.

A

A welcome to Sack.

SO soft streams meet, so streams with gladder
Meet after long divorcement by the Iles (smiles
When love the child of likenesse leadeth on
Their chrystall natures to an union.
So meet stoln kisses when the moon-shine nights
Call forth fierce lovers to their wisht delights.
So Kings and Queens meet when desire convinces
All thoughts but those that aime at getting Prin-
(ces,
As I meet thee soule of my life and fame
Eternall lamp of love, whose radiant flame
Out-stares the Heavens Osiris, and thy gleams
Darkens the splendour of his midday beames.
Welcome ô welcome my illustrious spouse,
Welcome as is the end unto my vowes.
Nay far more welcome then the happy soyl
The Sea-scourg'd Merchant after all his toyl
Salutes with tears of joy, when fires display
The smoaking chimnies of his Ithaca.
Where hast thou been so long from my embraces
Poor pittied exile, tell me did thy graces
Fly discontented hence, and for a time
Did rather chuse to blesse some other clime :
And

And was it to this end thou wentst to move me
More by thy absence to desire and love thee,
Why frowns my sweet? why does my Saint defer
Her bosome smiles from me her worshipper.
Why are those happy looks (the which have bin
Time past so fragant) sickly now drawn in
Like a dull twilight? tell me has my soul
Prophaned in speech, or done an act more foul
Against thy purer nature, for that fault
Ile expiate with fire, with haire, and salt,
And with the christall humor of the spring,
Purge hence the guilt, and aire, the quarrelling.
Wilt thou not smile, or tell me whats amisse,
Have I bin cold to hug thee, too remisse
And temperate in embracings? has desire
To thee-ward died in the embers, and no fire
Left in this rak'd up ash-heap as a mark
To testifie the glowing of a spark?
Have I divorc'd thee onely to combine
And quench my lust upon some other wine?
True I confesse I left thee, and appeal:
Twas done by me more to confirm my zeal
And double my affection, as doe those
Whose love grows more inflam'd by being foes.
But to forsake thee ever, could there be
A thought of such impossibility?
When thou thy self dost say thy Isles shall lack
Grapes, ere that *Herrick* leaves Canary Sack.
Thou art my life, my Heaven, salt to all
My dearest dainties, thou the principall

　　　　　　　　　　　　　Fire

Fire to all my functions, giv'ſt me blood,
Chine, ſpirit, and marrow and what elſe is good,
Thou mak'ſt me airy, active, to be borne
Like *Iphiclus* upon the tops of corne,
And mak'ſt me winged like the nimble Howers
To dance and caper on the heads of flowers,
And ride the Sunbeams. Can there be a thing
Under the heavenly Iſis that can bring
More love unto my life, or can preſent
My Genius with a fuller blandiſhment ?

A Parodox on the praiſe of a painted face.

NOt kiſſe by *Jove* I muſt and make impreſſion
As long as *Cupid* dares to hold his Seſſion
Upon thy fleſh and blood, our kiſſes ſhall
Outminute time, and without number fall.
Doe not I know theſe balls of bluſhing red
That on thy cheeks thus amorouſly are ſpred,
Thy ſnowy neck, thoſe veins upon thy brow
Which with their azure crinkling ſweetly bow,
Are from art borrowed, and no more thine own
Then chains that on St. *Georges* day are ſhown
Are proper to the wearer ? yet for this
I Idoll thee, and beg a courteous kiſſe.

H   The

The Fucus and Ceruffe which on thy face
The cunning hand doth lay to add more grace,
Deceive me with fuch pleafing fraud, that I
Find in thy art what can in nature lie :
Much like a Painter which upon fome wall
On which the cadent Sun-beams ufe to fall,
Paints with fuch art a guilded butterfly,
That filly maids with flow-made fingers try
To catch it, and then blufh at their miftake,
Yet of this painted fly much reckoning make.
Such is our ftate, fince what we look upon
Is nought but colour and proportion :
Give me a face that is as full of lies
As Gipfies or your cunning Lotteries ;
That is more falfe and more fophifticate
Then are your reliques, or a man of ftate :
Yet fuch being glazed by the flight of art
Gaine admiration, and win many a heart.
Put cafe there be a difference in the mould,
Yet may thy *Venus* be more brisk and bold.
—— for oftentimes we fee
Rich Candy wines in wooden bowles to be.
The odoriferous Civet doth not lye
Within the Muscats nofe, or eare, or eye,
But in a bafer place : for prudent nature
In drawing up the various forms and ftature,
Gives from the curious fhop of her large treafure
To faire parts comelineffe, to bafer pleafure.
The faireft flower that in the fpring doth grow
Is not fo much for ufe, as for a fhow.

                                                    As

As Lillies, Hyacinths, the gorgeous birth
Of all pied flowers which diaper the earth,
Please more with their discolour'd purple traine
Then wholefom potherbs which for use remaine.
Should I a golden speckled Serpent kisse
Because the colour which he wears is his?
A perphum'd cordovain who would not wear,
Because its sent is borrowed otherwhere?
The cloths and vestiments which grace us all
Are not our own but adventitiall.
Time rifles natures beauty, but fly art
Repaires by cunning each decaied part,
Fills here a wrinkle, and there purles a veine;
And with a cunning hand runs ore againe
The breaches dented by the pen of time,
And makes deformity to be no crime.
So when great men are gnip'd by sicknesse hand,
Illustrious phisick pregnantly doth stand
To patch up foule diseases, and doth strive
To keep their tottering carkases alive.
Beauty a candle is, with every puffe
Blown out, leaves nothing but a stinking snuffe
To fill our noftrils with; thus boldly think
The purest candle yields the foulest stink:
As the pure food, and daintiest nutriment,
Yields the most strong and hottest excrement.
Why hang we then on things so apt to vary,
So fleeting, brittle, and so temporary,
That agues, coughs, the toothach, or cathar,
Slight touches of diseases spoil and mar.

But when that age their beauty doth displace,
And plows up furrows in their once smooth face ;
Then they become forsaken and do show
Like stately Abbies destroyed long ago.
Love grant me then a reparable face,
That whilst there colours are can want no grace :
Pygmalions painted statue I could love,
If it were warme, and soft, or could but move.

A Song.

WHen *Orpheus* swetly did complain
        Upon his Lute with heavy strain
How his *Euridice* was slain ;
            The trees to hear
            Obtain'd an eare
And after left it off again.

At every stroke and every stay
The boughs kept time and nodding lay,
And listned bending every way ;
            The ashen tree
            As well as well as he
Began to shake and learnt to play.

If

If wood could ſpeak, a tree might hear,
If wood can ſound our griefe ſo near,
A tree might drop an amber tear :
     If wood ſo well
     Could ſound a knell,
The Cypreſſe might condoal the bear

The ſtanding nobles of the grove,
Hearing dead wood to ſpeak and move,
The fatall axe began to love ;
     They envied death
     That gave ſuch breath,
As men alive doe Saints above.

Upon Mr. Hoptons *death.*

GRiefs prodigals where are you? unthrifts wher?
  Whoſe tears and ſighs extemporary are ;
Pour'd out, not ſpent, who never ask a day
Your debt of ſorrow on the grave to pay ;
But as if one hours mourning could ſuffice,
Dare think it now no ſin to have dry eyes :
Away, profane not *Hoptons* death, nor ſhame
His grave with griefe not worthy of that name :
Sorrow conceiv'd and vented both together;
Like prayers of Puritans, or in foul weather

H 3   The

The sailers sore't devotion, when in fear
They pray this minute, and the next they swear.
No I must meet with men, men that doe know
How to compute their tears and weigh their wo,
That can set down in an exact account
To what the losse of *Hopton* doth amount:
Tell you particulars, how much of truth
Of unmatch'd virtue and untainted youth
Is gone with him, and having sum'd all look
Like bankrupt Merchants on their table book,
With eyes confounded and amaz'd to find
The poor and blanck remainder left behind.

On his Mistresse eye.

AM I once more blest with a grace so high
As to be lookt on with that other eye?
Or shall I think it once more sent againe
To iterate my souls sweet lasting paine?
Your other eye, dear soule, had fire before
And darts enough, you need not have sought more
From this revived; scarce could I endure
The lustre of this eye when 'twas obscure:
How shall I now when like a fresh-born Sun
It strikes forth such a new reflection?
Yet welcome, dearest torment, spare not me (thee
Dart forth more flames, the, please if sent from

I

I hope your eyes as they in lustre doe,
Will imitate the Sun in virtue too.
If plagues and sicknesses from him be sent (ment.
Yet gives he warmth, life, growth and nourish-
This is my comfort now, if one eye strike,
The other may give remedy alike.
Welcome againe clear lamp of beauty, shine,
Shine bright on Earth as do the soules divine,
To which my thoughts with like devotion run
As *Indians* adore the rising Sun.
Now shall I mine own Image view alive
In this extenuating perspective,
This living looking glasse, when thou sha't grace
Me, sweet, so much as to admire my face
Neighbour to thine, o how I then shall love
To see my shape in that black stream to move:
Against all reason I then more admire
My shadow there, then my whole selfe entire.
How oft (though loth from that sweet seat to part)
Strive I to travell that way to thy heart;
Where if one wink doe thy quick look recall,
I loose, poor wretch, my shadow, selfe, and all.
Thus all the life which I so glorious thought
By thy sole wink is quencht and turn'd to nought
Oh how I wont to curse that cobweb lawn
Which like a curtaine ore thy eye was drawn,
As if that death upon that eye did sit,
And this had bin the winding sheet for it,
The which, as it from off that eye was thrown,
Seemd to look pale for griefe that it was gone.

Yet

Yet when both this and t'other dainty robe
Did close like cases that moſt heavenly globe,
Think not they could diſparage your faire eyes;
No more then painters doe their chiefeſt prize,
Who uſe to hang ſome veil or ſilken ſheet,
That men may more deſire and long to ſe't.

To Dr. Griffith *heald of a ſtrange cure by* Bernard Wright *of* Oxford.

WElcome abroad, ô welcome from your (bed
    I joy to ſee you thus delivered.
After four years in travell iſſues forth
A birth of laſting wonder, whereat truth
Might well ſuſpect her ſelfe, a new diſeaſe
Borne to advance the Surgeons of our dayes
Above all others: a perfidious bone
Eaten and undermind by humours growr.:
Lodg'd in the captive thigh, which firſt of any
Halted, yet furniſht with a bone to many;
No Golgotha, nor charnell houſe, nor field,
If all were ſearcht could ſuch another yield,
A bone ſo lockt and hugd, as is a bar
That back and forward may be wreſted far
But not puld out at either hole, nor could
The cunning workman come to 't as he would:

Croſſe

Croffe veins did guard the fore, a hollow cave
Muft wade into the flefh, the Surgeons grave
Thus being digd, the file without delay
Muft grate the bone, and carve thofe chips away.
Bleft be the midmen whofe dexterity
Puld ont a birth like *Bacchus* from the thigh.
Tutors of nature, whofe well guided art
Can rectifie her wants in every part:
Who by preferving others pay the debt
They owe to nature, and doe rebeget
Her ftrength grown ruinate : I could be glad
Such liv'd the dayes which they to others add :
Nor can I rightly tell the happier man
The patient or the Surgeon ; doe but fcan
His praife thy eafe, 'twas fure an extafie
That kild *Van-otto* not a lethargy ;
Striving to crown his work he bravely tryed
His laft and greateft cure then gladly dyed.
Bernard muft tarry longer ; fhould he flye
After his brother all the world muft dye
Or live a cripple ; *Griffiths* happy fate
Requires the fame hand ftill to iterate
No leffe a miracle : the joyners skill
Could never mend his carved pate fo well
As he hath heald a naturall : the ftout
And boafting *Paracelfus* who gives out
His rule can give mans life eternity,
Would faintly doubt of his recovery ;
He that hath wrought thefe cures I think he can
As well of fcraps make up a perfect man.

Oh

Oh had you seen his marrow drop away,
Or the others brains drop out, then would you say
Nothing could cure this fracture or that bone
Save *Bernard* or the Resurrection.
Now smile upon thy torment, pretty thing
How will you use it ? bury it in a ring
Like a deaths head, or send it to the grave
In earnest of the body it must have :
Or if you will you may the same translate
Into a die because 'twas fortunate ;
The ring were blest, 'tis like a Diamond born
Out of a Rock, so was it hewn and torn
Out of your thigh : the gem worth nothing is
Untill it be cut forth, no more is this.
Happy are you that know what treasure 'tis
To find lost health, they onely feel the blisse:
Thou that hast felt these pains, must wel maintain
Mans chiefest pleasure is but want of pain.
Enjoy thy selfe ; for nothing worse can come
To one so schoold and vers'd in martyrdome.

The

The Liberty and Requiem of an imprisoned Royalist.

BEat on proud billows, *Boreas* blow
swell'd curled Waves high as *Joves* roof,
Your incivility shall know,
That innocence is tempest proof.   (calm,
Though surly *Nereus* frown, my thoughts are
Then strike (afflictions) for your wounds are balm.

That which the world miscalls a jaile,
A private closet is to me,
Whilst a good conscience is my baile,
And innocence my liberty.
Locks, bars, walls, lonenesse, tho together met,
Make me no prisoner, but an Anchoret.

I, whilst I wisht to be retir'd,
Into this private room was turn'd
As if their wisdomes had conspir'd
A Salamander should be burn'd:
And like those Sophies who would drown a fish,
I am condemn'd to suffer what I wish.

The

The Cynick hug his poverty,
The Pelicane her wildernesse,
And 'tis the *Indians* pride to lye
Naked on frozen *Cuncasus*.
And like to these, Stoicks severe we see
Make torments easie by their apathy.

These manicles upon my arme
I as my sweethearts favours wear,
And then to keep my ancles warm
I have some Iron shackles there :
These walls are but my garrison, this Cell
Which men call Jaile, doth prove my Citadell

So he that strook at *Jasons* life,
Thinking h' had made his purpose sure,
By a malicious friendly knife,
Did onely wound him to a cure.
Malice I see wants wit, for what is meant
Mischiefe, oft times proves favour by th' event.

I'me in this Cabinet lockt up
Like some high prized Margarite ;
Or like some great Mogul, or Pope,
Am cloyster'd up from publique sight :
Retir'dnesse is a part of majesty,
And thus, proud *Sultan*, I'me as great as thee.

Here

Here fin for want of food doth ftarve,
 Where tempting objects are not feen,
 And thefe walls doe onely ferve
 To keep vice out, not keep me in.
Malice of late's grown charitable fure,
I'me not committed, but am kept fecure.

 When once my Prince affliction hath,
 Profperity doth treafon feem,
 And then to fmooth fo rough a path
 I can learn patience too from him.
Now not to fuffer fhews no loyall heart, (fmart.
When Kings want eafe fubjects muft love to

 What tho I cannot fee my King
 Either in's perfon or his coyne,
 Yet contemplation is a thing
 Which renders what I have not mine.
My King from me no Adamant can part,
Whom I doe wear ingraven in my heart.

 My foul's free, as th' ambient aire,
 Altho my bafer part's immur'd,
 Whilft loyall thoughts doe ftill repaire
 T' accompany my folitude.
And though rebellion doe my body bind,
My King can onely captivate my mind.

                              Have

Have you not seen the Nightingale
When turn'd a Pilgrim to a cage,
How she doth sing her wonted tile
In that her narrow hermitage ;
Even there her chanting melody doth prove
That all her bars are trees, her cage a grove

I am that bird, which they combine
Thus to deprive of liberty,
Who though they doe my corps confine,
Yet maugre hate my soule is free :
And tho immur'd, yet can I chirp and sing
Disgrace to rebells, glory to my King.

To his imperious Mistresse.

WEll, well 'tis true,
     I am now fal'n in love,
   And 'tis with you,
And now I plainly see,
While you'r enthron'd by me above
You all your art and power improve
   To tyrannize ore me,
And make my flames the objects of your scorn,
While you rejoyce, and feast your eyes, to see me
                              (quite forlorn.

                                        But

But yet be wife,
And don't believe that I
   Doe think your eyes
  More bright than Stars can be,
Or that you Angels far out-vy
In their Cœleſtiall livery
   Twas all but Poetry.
I could have ſaid as much by any ſhe,
You are no beauty of your ſelfe, but are made ſo
                                   (by me.

   Though we like fools
Fathome the Earth and sky,
   And drain the Schools
  For names t' expreſſe you by,
Out-rend all loud hyperbolyes
To dub our fancies Deityes
   By *Cupids* heraldry ;
We know you'r fleſh and blood as well as men,
And when we pleaſe can mortalize, and make you
                                   (ſo agen.

   Yet ſince my fate
Hath drawn me to the thing
   Which I did hate,
  Ile not my labour looſe ;
But will love, and as I begin
To the purpoſe, now my hand is in,
   Spight of the art you uſe :
And have you know the world is not ſo bare ;
Ther's things enough to love beſides ſuch toyes
                              (as **Ladies** are.
                                         I'le

I'le love good wine,
I'le love my book and muſe,
   Nay all the nine ;
  I'le love my reall friend :
I'le love my horſe ; and could I chuſe
One that my love would not abuſe,
   To her my love ſhould bend.
I will love thoſe that laugh, and thoſe that ſing,
Ile never pine my ſelfe away for any female thing.

On Dr. Ravis *Biſhop of* London.

WHen I paſs'd *'Pauls* and traveld on the
                    (walk
Where all our *Brittain* ſinners ſwear and talk :
Old *Harry Ruffians,* Bankrupts, and South-ſayers,
And youths whoſe couſenage is as old as theirs :
And there beheld the body of my Lord
Trod under foot of vice which he abhord ;
It griev'd me that the Landlord of all times
Should ſet long lives and leaſes to their crimes,
And to his ſpringing honours ſhould afford
Scarce ſo much Sun as to the prophets gourd :
But ſince ſwift flights of vertue have good ends,
Like breath of Angells which a bleſſing ſends
                        And

And vanisheth withall, whilst fouler deeds
Expect a tedious harvest for bad seeds.
I blame not fame and nature, if they gave
Where they could give no more, their last a grave;
And justly doe thy grieved friends forbear
Marble and Alabaster boyes to rear
Ore thy Religious dust, because they know
Thy worth, which such allusions cannot shew,
For thou hast trod amongst those happy ones,
Who trust not in their superscriptions,
Their hired Epitaphs and perjur'd stone,
Which so belies the soule when she is gone :
Thou doest commit thy body as it lies
To tongues of living men, not unborn eyes ;
What profits then a sheet of lead ? what good
If on thy coarse a Marble quarry stood ?
Let those that fear their rising purchase vaults,
And rear them statues to excuse their faults ;
As if like birds that peck at Painters grapes,
The judg knew not their persons from their shapes.
Nor needs the Chancelor boast, whose Pyramis
Above the House and Altar reared is ;
For though thy body fill a viler room,
Thou shalt not change deeds with him for his
                                        (tomb

I   O2

On Dr. Langton.

BEcause of fleshy mould we be
Subject unto mortality ;
Let no man wonder at his death,
More flesh he had, and then lesse breath :
But if you question how he dyed
Twas not the fall of swelling pride,
Twas no ambition to ascend
Heaven in humility : his end
Assured us his God did make
This piece for our example sake.
Had you but seen him in his way
To Church his last best Sabbath day,
His strugling soule did make such hast
As if each breath should be his last ;
Each stone he trod on sinking strove
To make his grave, and showed his love :
O how his sweating body wept,
Knowing how soon it should be swept
Ith' mould ; but while he steals to pray,
His weighty members long to stay,
Each word did bring a breathlesse tear,
As if he'd leave his spirit there :

He

He gone looks back as twere to see
The place where he would buried be,
Bowing as if did desire
At the same time for to expire:
Wh ch being done he long shall dwell
Within the place he loved so well ;
Where night and morning hundreds come
A Pilgrimage unto his tomb.

To the Bell-Founder of great Tom of Christ-Church in Oxford.

THou that by ruine doest repaire,
And by destruction art a Founder
  Whose art doth tell us what men are,
Who by corruption shalt rise founder ;
  In this fierce fires intensive heat,
  Remember this is Tom the great.

  And, Cyclops, think at every stroak
With which thy sledge his side shall wound,
  That then some Statute thou hast broak
Which long depended on his sound ;
  And that our Colledge-Gates doe cry
  They were not shut since Tom did die.

I 2   Think

Think what a scourge 'tis to the City
To drink and swear by *Carfax* Bell,
  Which bellowing without tune or pitty
The night and day devides not well;
    But the poor tradesmen must give ore
    His ale at eight or sit till four.

We all in hast drink off our wine,
As if we never should drink more;
  So that the reckoning after nine
Is larger now then that before.
    Release this tongue which erst could say
    Home Scollers; drawer whats to pay?

So thou of order shalt be Founder,
Making a Ruler for the people,
  One that shalt ring thy praises rounder
Then t'other six bells in the steeple:
    Wherefore think when Tom is running
    Our manners wait upon thy cunning.

Then let him raised be from ground
The same in number, weight, and sound;
For may thy conscience rule thy gaine,
Or would thy theft might be thy baine.

On

On a Gentleman, that kiſſing
his Miſtreſſe left blood
upon her.

WHat myſtery is this that I ſhould find
    My blood in kiſſing you to ſtay behind?
Twas not for want of colour that required
My blood for paint : no die could be deſired
On that faire cheeck, where ſcarlet were a ſpot,
And where the juice of Lillies but a blot :
If at the preſence of the murtherer
The wound will bleed, and tell the cauſe is there,
A touch will doe much more : even ſo my heart
When ſecretly it felt your killing dart   (plain
Shewed it in blood ; which yet doth more com-
Becauſe it cannot be ſo toucht again.
This wounded heart to ſhew its love moſt true
Sent forth a drop and wrote its mind on you ;
Was ever paper halfe ſo white as this,
Or wax ſo yielding to the printed kiſſe ?
Or ſeal ſo ſtrong ? no letter ere was writ
That could the Authors mind ſo truly fit :
For though my ſelfe to forraine countries fly
My blood deſires to keep you company ;

         Here

Here I could fpill it all, thus I can free
My enemy from blood though flaine I be :
But flaine I cannot be, nor meet with ill,
Since but to you I have no blood to fpill.

On an aged Gentlewoman.

NO fpring nor fummers beauty hath fuch
    As I have feen in one autumnall face. (grace
Young beauties force their loves, and thats a rape,
Your's doth, but counfell, yet they cannot fcape :
If 'twere a fhame to love, here twere no fhame,
Affection takes here reverences name.
Were her firft years the golden age ? thats true;
But now fhe's gold oft tried and ever new :
That was her torrid and inflaming time,
This is her tolerable tropick clime.   (thence,
Faire eyes, who afkes more heat then comes from
He in a feaver wifhes peftilence.
Call not thofe wrinkles graves,if graves they were
They were loves graves,for elf they are no where.
Yet lies not love dead here, but here doth fit
Vowed to this trench like to an Anchoret :
And here till her (which muft be his) death's
He doth not dig a grave,but build a tomb:(doom
Here dwells he, though he fojourne every where
In progreffe, yet his ftanding houfe is here.
                                           fhe

She allwayes evening is, nor noon nor night,
Where's no voluptuousnsse, though a delight.
Xerxes strange love, the broad-leav'd plantane
Was loved for age, none being so large as she(tree,
Or else because being young, nature did blesse
Her youth with ages glory barrennesse.
If we love things long sought, age is a thing
Which we are sixty years a compassing :
If transitory things which soon'decay,
Age must be loveliest at the latest day.
But name not winter-faces, whose skin's slack,
Lank like an unthrifts purse, or empty sack ;
Whose eyes seek light within, for all here's shade,
Whose mouth's a hole rather worn out then made,
Whose severall tooth to a severall place is gone
To vex their soules at the Resurrection :
Name not these living deaths-heads unto me,
For such not antient, but antiques be.
I hate extreams ; yet I had rather stay
With tombs then cradles to wear out the day :
Since that loves naturall motion is may still
My love descend and journey down the hill ;
Not panting after growing beauties, so
I shall ebb on with them that homewards go.

I 4   *On*

On his Mistresse going to Sea.

FArewell fair Saint, may not the Seas and wind
Swel like the heart and eyes you leave behind,
But calme and gentle (like the looks they bear)
Smile on your face and whisper in your eare :
Let no foule billow offer to arise
That it may nearer look upon your eyes,
Leaſt wind and waves enamourd with such form
Should throng and croud themselves into a ſtorm;
But if it be your fate (vaſt Seas) to love,
Of my becalmed heart learn how to move :
Move then, but in a gentle lovers pace,
No wrinkles nor no furrowes in your face ;
And ye fierce winds see that you tell your tale
In such a breath as may but fill her ſaile :
So whilſt you court her each his ſeverall way
You will her ſafely to her port convay ;
And looſe her in a noble way of woing,
Whilſt both contribute to your own undoing.

A

A Copy of Verses spoke to King
CHARLES *by way of entertainment
when he was pleas'd to grace S.*
John's *Colledge with his
visit.* 1 6 3 6.

WEre they not Argells sang, did not mine
    eares
Drink in a sacred Anthem from yon sphears?
Was I not blest with *Charles* and *Maries* name,
Names wherein dwells all Musick? tis the same.
Hark, I my self now but speak *Charles* and *Mary*,
And 'tis a Poem, nay 'tis a library.

All haile to your dread Majesties, whose power
Adds lustre to our feast, and to our bower:
And what place fitter for so Royall guests
Then this, where every book presents a feast.
Here's *Virgils* well-drest Venison, here's the wine
Made *Horace* sing so sweetly; here you dine
With the rich *Cleopatra's* warelike love;
Nay you may feast and frolick here with *Jove*.
Next view that bower, which is as yet all green,
But when you'r there, the red and white are seen.
A bower, which had (tis true) been beautified
With catechising Arras on each side;

                        But

But we the Baptists sons did much desire
To have it like the dwelling of our sire
A grove or desart. See (dread Leige) youle guesse
Even our whole Colledge in a wildernesse.
Your eyes and eares being fed, tast of that feast,
Which hath its pomp and glory from its guest.

Upon the new Quadrangle of St. Johns Colledge in Oxford, built by the most Reverend Father in God the Lord Archbishop of Canterbury.

'Tis done, and now wheres he that cryed it
      For the long tedious businesse of the (down
Let him but see it thus, and heel contend (Town,
How we could such a Quadrat so soon end,
Nay think 'twas time little enough to frame
The exact modell onely of the same.
Tis finish'd then ; and so, there's not the eye
Can blame it, thats best skilld in Symmetry :
You'd think each stone were rais'd by *Orpheus* art,
There's such sweet harmony in every part.
Thus they are one : yet if you please to pry
But farther in the quaint variety
Of the choise workmen, there will seem to be
A disagreeing uniformity.
Here Angels, stars, there vertues arts are seen,
And in whom all these meet the King and Queen.
                                          Next

Next view the smoothfaced columns, and each one
Looks like a pile of well joynd Punice-stone :
Nor wonder, for as smooth, as cleare they are
As is your Mistresse glasse, or what shines there.
So that you'd think at first sight at a blush
The massy solid earth Diaphanous.
But these are common, would you see that thing
In which our King delights, which in our King ?
Look up, and then with reverence cast your eye
Upon our *Maryes* comely Majesty :
Tis she, and yet had you her self ere seen, (Queen.
You'd swear but for the crown 'twere not the
Nor all the workmans fault ; for what can be
I would faine know like to a Deity ?
Unlesse her *Charles* ; yet hath his statue proved
So like himselfe you'd think it spoke and mov'd,
But that you plainely see tis brasse ; nay were
The Guard but near, they'd cry the King, be bare.
Rare forme, and as rare matter ; that can give
Our *Charles* after his reigne ages to live.
Not like your graver Citizens wise cost,
Who think they have King enough on a sign-post:
Where he may stand (for all I see) unknown,
But for the loving superscription.
No ; here he reigns in state, to every eye
So like himselfe in compleat Majesty,
That men shall cry, viewing his limbs and face
All fresh three ages hence, long live his Grace.
    Blest be that subject then, which did foresee
The Kings (though he's as God) mortality :

                            And

And through a Princely care hath found the way
To reinthrone his dutt and crown his clay ;
That fo what ftrange events foere may fall
Through peace or war antimonarchical :　(flame
Though thefe three Kingdoms fhould becom one
And that confume us with our King and his name ;
Yet here our gracious *Charles* whenever lent
To his much honourd Marble, and there fpent
To a dutt's atome, being then fcarce a thing,
May ftill reigne on, and long furvive a King.

Fortunes Legacy.

BLind fortune if thou wants a guide ;
Ile fhew thee how thou fhalt divide,
Diftribute unto each his due :
Juftice is blind and fo are you.
Toth' Uferer this doom impart,
May Scriveners break and then his heart ;
His debters all to beggery call,
Or whats as bad turne Courtiers all.
Unto the tradefmen that fell dear
A long Vacation all the year,
Revenge us too for their deceits
By fending wives light as their weights.
But fortune how wilt recompence
The Frenchmens daily infolence ?

That

That they may know no greater paine
May they returne to *France* againe.
To lovers, that will not beleeve
Their sweet mistakes, thy blindnesse give.
And least the Players should grow poor
Give them *Aglaura's* more and more.
To Phisitians if thou please
Give them another new disease.
To Schollers give (if thou canst doe't)
A Benefice without a suit.
To court Lords grant monopolies,
And to their wives communities :
So fortune thou shalt please them all,
When Lords doe rise and Ladies fall.
Give to the Lawers I beseech
As much for silence as for speech.
Give Ladies Ushers strength of back,
And unto me a cup of Sack.

Upon

Upon a Gentlewomans enter-
tainment of him.

WHether, sweet Mistresse, I should most
    Commend your Musick or your cott :
Your well spread table, or the choise
Banquet of your hand and voyce,
There's none will doubt. For can there be
Twixt earth and Heaven analogy ?
Or shall a trencher or dish stand
In competition with your hand ?
Your hand, that turns men all to eare :
Your hand, whose every joynts a sphear.
For certainly he that shall see
The swiftnesse of your harmony,
Will streightwayes in amazement prove
The spheares to you but slowly move ;
And in that thought confesse that thus
The Heavens are come down to us.
As he may well ; when he shall hear
Such Aires as may be sung even there ;

                                    Your

Your sacred Anthems, strains that may
Grace the eternall Quire to play :
And certainly they were prepar'd
By Angells onely to be heard,
Then happy I that was so blest
To be yours and your Musicks guest ;
For which Ide change all other chear,
Thinking the best though given to dear.
For yours are delicates that fill,
And filling leave us empty still :
Sweetmeats that surfet to delight,
Whose fullnesse is meere appetite.
Then farewell all our heavenly fare,
Those singing dainties of the aire ;
For you to me doe seem as good
As all the conforts of the wood ;
And might I but enjoy my choice,
My Quire should be your onely voyce.

To

To a black Gentlewoman Mistresse A. H.

GRieve not (faire maid) cause you are black ;
                                    (so's she
Thats spouse to him who died upon the tree :
And so is every thing. For to your thought,
If you but wink, the worlds as dark as nought.
Or doe but look abroad and you shall meet
In every hallowed Church, in every street,
The fairest still in this ; who think they lack
Of their perfections if not all in black :   (necks,
Their gowns, their veiles are so, nay more their
Their very beauties are foild off with specks
Of the dark colour. Whilst thus to her mate
Each seems more faire. Now they but personate
What you are really. Your fairest haire
Shadows the Picture of your face more faire :
Your two black sphears are like twoGlobes beset
With Ebony, or ring'd about with Jet.
O how I now desire ene to depart
From all the rest, and study the Black art :
But since thats not alowed me, I will see
How I may truely, fairest, study thee.

                                    To

To the Memory of
BEN: JOHNSON.

AS when the vestall hearth went out, no fire
Lesse hoiy then the flame that did expire
Could kindle it againe : so at thy fall
Our wit great *Ben*, is too Apocriphall
To celebrate the losse ; since tis too much
To write thy Epitaph, and not be such.
What thou wert, like the hard Oracles of old
Without an extasie cannot be told.
We must be ravisht first, thou must infuse
Thy selfe into us both the theam and muse.
Else, though we all conspir'd to make thy herse
Our work, so that it had been but one great verse :
Though the Priest had translated for that time
The Liturgy, and buried thee in rime ;
So that in meeter we had heard it said
Poetique dust is to Poetique laid :   (mighst have
And though that dust being *Shakespears*, thou
Not his room but the Poet for thy grave ;
So that as thou didst Prince of numbers dye
And live, so now thou mighst in numbers lye ;
Twere fraile solemnity. Verses on thee
And not like thine, would but kind libels be;(raise
And we, not speaking thy whole worth, should
Worse blots then they that envied thy praise.

         K   Indeed

Indeed thou needſt not us, ſince above all
Invention, thou wert thine own funerall.
Hereafter when time hath fed on thy Tomb,
The inſcription worne out, and the marble dumb;
So that 'twould poſe a Critick to reſtore
Halfe words, and words expir'd ſo long before.
When thy maim'd ſtatue hath a ſentenc'd face,
And looks that are the horrour of the place;
That twill be learning and antiquity
To ask a *Selden* to ſay this was thee;   (fear
Thou'lt have a whole name ſkill: nor needſt thou
That will be ruind, or looſe noſe or hair.
Let others write ſo thin, that they can't be
Authors till rotten, no poſterity   (then
Can add to thy works, th' had their whole growth
When firſt borne, and came aged from the pen.
Whilſt living thou enjoyeſt the fame and ſence,
And all that time gives but the reverence.
When tha'rt of *Homers* years, no man will ſay
Thy Poems are leſſe worthy, but more gray.
Tis baſtard Poetry, and of the falſe blood
Which can't withot ſucceſſion be good.
Things that will always laſt, doe thus agree
With things Eternall, they at once perfect be.
Scorne then their cenſure, who gave out thy wit
As long about a Comedy did ſit,
As Elephants bring forth; and that thy blots
And mendings took more time then *Fortune* plots:
That ſuch thy drought was, and ſo great thy thirſt,
That all thy Plays were drawn at the Mermaid firſt.

                                        That

That the Kings yearly Butt wrote, and his wine
Had more right then thou to thy Cateline.
Let such men keep a diet, let their wit
Be rackt,and while they write,suffer a fit (gouur,
When they have felt tortures which outpaine the
Such as with lesse thestate draws Treafon out;(lie,
Though they should the length of consumption
Sick of their Verfe, and of their Poem die,
Twould not be thy worft Scene, but would at laft
Confirme their boaftings,and shew't made in haft.
He that writes well, writes quick,fince the rules
Nothing is flowly done,thats always new. (true,
So when thy Fox had ten times Acted been,
Each day was firft,but that twas cheaper feen.
And to thy Alchymift Played ore and ore,(door
Was new oth' ftage, when twas not at the
We, like the Actors, did repeat, the pit
The firft time faw, the next conceived thy wit :
Which wascaft in thofe forms,fuch rules,fuch arts,
That but to fome not halfe thy Acts were parts :
Since of fome filken judgements we may fay
They fild a box two houres, but faw no Play.
So that the unlearned loft their mony, and
Schollers faved onely, that could underftand.
Thy Scene was free from monfters, no hard plot
Calld down a God t' untie the unlikely knot.
The ftage was ftill a ftage, two entrances
Were not two parts of the world disjoynd by Seas
Thine were land Tragedies, no Prince was found
To fwim a wholeScene out,the noth'ftagedrownd,

Pitcht fields, and Red-Bul wars, still felt thy doom,
Thou laidst no sieges to the Musick Room;
Nor wouldst alow to thy best Comedies
Humors that should above the people rise:
Yet was thy language and thy stile so high
Thy Sock to the ancle, Buskin reachd doth' thigh:
And both so chast, so 'bove dramatick clean,
That we both safely saw and lived thy Scene
No foul loose line did prostitute thy wit,
Thou wrotst thy Comedies, didst not commit:
We did the vice arraignd not tempting hear,
And were made judges not bad parts by the care.
For thou even sin didst in such words array,
That some who came bad parts, went out good
Which ended not with th' Epilogue, the age of Play.
Still Acted, and grew innocent from the stage.
Tis true thou hadst some sharpnesse, but thy salt
Serv'd but with pleasure to reforme the fault:
Men were laught into vertue, and none more
Hated *Face* acted then were such before.
So did thy sting not blood but humors draw;
So much doth Satyre more correct then Law;
Which was not nature in thee, as some call
Thy teeth, who say thy wit lay in thy gall.
That thou dist quarrel first, and then in spight
Didst 'gainst a person of such vices write:
And twas revenge not truth, that on the stage
Carlo was not presented, but thy rage:
And that when thou in company wert met,
Thy meat took notes, and thy discourse was net.

                                                We

We know thy free vaine had this innocence,
To spare the party, and to brand the offence.
And the just indignation thou wert in
Did not expose *Shift* but his tricks and gin.

(these

Thou might have us'd th'old comick freedome,
Might have seen themselves played like *Socrates*.
Like *Cleon Mammon* might the Knight have been;
If as Greek Authors thou hadst turn'd Greek
And hadst not chosen rather to translate (spleen;
Their learning into English, not their hate.
Indeed this last, if thou hadst been bereft
Of thy humanity, might be called theft.
The other was not, whatsoere was strange
Or borrowed in thee did grow thine by th'

(change.

Who without Latine helps, hadst been as rare
As *Beaument*, *Fletcher*, or as *Shakespeare* were :
And like them from thy native stock couldst say
Poets and Kings are not born every day.

K 3　　　　　　*An*

An Anſwer to the Letter of the Cloake.

Mr. Roberts,

I Wonder that you ſhould ſend for the Cloak,
I thought you ſcornd it ſhould be ſpoke
That once your promiſe ſhould be broke,
If from your word you doe revoke
I have wit enough to keep the Cloak.

You ſay youle make me ſmart for the Cloak,
I doe not care a fart for the Cloak,
Yet I will ſtudy the black art in the Cloak
Rather then I will part with the Cloak.

You ſay you mean to try for the Cloak,
I ſcorne to tell a lie for the Cloak,
My word Ile never deny for the Cloak
Although I thought youd cry for the Cloak.

I doe proteſt moſt deep in the Cloak
I did both mourne and weep in the Cloak,
And if I ſhould not keep the Cloak
I were a very ſheep in the Cloak.

I

I took your Cloak to mourne in your Cloak,
My corps I did adorne in your Cloak,
And many a time have I sworn in your Cloak
That I will never return in your Cloak.

Your father we did bury in the Cloak,
And after we were merry in the Cloak,
And then I told Mr. *Perry* of the Cloak,
And yet I am not weary of the Cloak.

Yet still I stand in fear of the Cloak
That I shall be never the near for the Cloak:
I pray you, good Sir, forbear the Cloak
I know that you can spare the Cloak.

It cost me many a tear in your Cloak,
And many a beaker of bear in your Cloak,
And yet I stand in fear of your Cloak
That I shall be nere the near for your Cloak.

Therefore, good Sir, forbear the Cloak,
For though I have worn bare the Cloak,
I had rather for to tear the Cloak
Then see another wear the Cloak.
    Your friend in truth till death me choak
    If you will let me have the Cloak.

K 4   *Loves*

Loves Courtship.

Hark my *Flora*, Love doth call us
To the strife that must befall us :
He hath rob'd his mothers Myrtles,
And hath puld her downy Turtles.
    See our geniall posts are crownd,
And our beds like billowes rise :
    Softer lifts are no where found,
And the strife its selfe's the prize.

Let not shades and dark affright thee,
Thy eyes have lustre that will light thee :
Think not any can surprize us,
Love himselfe doth now disguise us :
    From thy waft that girdle throw
Night and silence both wait here,
    Words or actions who can know
Where there's neither eye nor eare.

Shew thy bosome and then hide it,
Licence touching and then chide it ;
Profer something and forbear it,
Give a grant and then forswear it :

                                            Ask

Ask where all my shame is gone,
Call us wanton wicked men ;
   Doe as Turtles kisse and grone,
Say thou nere shalt joy againe.

I can hear thee curse, yet chase thee ;
Drink thy tears and still embrace thee :
Easie riches are no treasure,
She thats willing spoiles the pleasure :
   Love bids learn the wrestlers slight,
Pull and struggle when we twine ;
   Let me use my force to night,
The next conquest shall be thine.

Upon the death of the Lord Stafford, *the last of his name.*

Must then our loves be short still ? must we
  Not to enjoy? only admire & loose? (chuse
Must axiomes hence grow sadly understood,
And we thus see tis dangerous to be good ?
So books begun are broken off, and we
Receive a fragment for an History ;
And as 'twere present wealth, what was but debt,
Lose that of which we are not owners yet ;
                     But

But as in books that want the cloſing line,
We onely can conjecture, and repine :
So muſt we here too onely grieve, and gueſſe,
And by our fancy make, whats wanting, leſſe.
Thus when rich webs are left unfiniſhed,
The ſpider doth ſupply them with her thred.
For tell me what addition can be wrought
To him, whoſe youth was even the bound of
                                    (thought.
Whoſe buddings did deſerve the robe, whiles we
In ſmoothneſſe did the deeds of wrinkles ſee :
                                    (fit.
When his State-nonage might have been thought
To break the cuſtome and allowed to ſit.
His actions veiled his age, and could not ſtay
For that we call ripeneſſe, and juſt day.
Others may wait the ſtaffe and the gray haire,
And call that wiſdome which is onely feare.
Chriſten a coldneſſe temperance, and then boaſt
Full and ripe vertue, when all actions loſt :
This is not to be noble, but be ſlack ;
A *Stafford* ne're was good by the Almanack.
He, who thus ſtayes the ſeaſon, and expects,
Doth not gaine habits, but diſguiſe defects.
Here nature outſlips culture : he came tried,
Straight of himſelfe at firſt, not rectified :
Manners ſo pleaſing and ſo handſome caſt,
That ſtill that overcame which was ſhewn laſt.
All minds were captived thence, as if 't had been
The ſame to him to have been loved and ſeen.

                                    Had

Had he not been fnatch'd thus, what drive hearts
Into his nets, would have driven Cities too: (now
For thefe his effayes which began to win (within.
Were but bright fparks which fhewed the mine
Rude draughts unto the Picture ; things we may
Stile the firft beams of the increafing day ;
Which did but onely great difcoveries bring,
As outward coolenefle fhews the inward fpring.
Nor were his actions to content the fight,
Like Artifts pieces plac'd in a good light,
That they might take at diftance, and obtrude
Something unto the eye that might delude :
His deeds did all moft perfect then appear
When you obferv'd, view'd clofe, and did ftand
                                                  (near
For could there ought elfe fpring from him whofe
                                                  (line
From which he fprung was rule and difcipline.
Whofe vertues were as books before him fet,
So that they did inftruct, who did beget :
Taught thence not to be powerfull, but know,
Shewing he was their blood by living fo.
For whereas fome are by their big-lip known,
Others by imprinted burning fwords werethown ;
                                                  (fame
So they by great deeds are, from which bright
Engraves free reputation on their name :
Thefe are their native marks, and it hath been
The *Staffords* lot to have their fignes within.
                                                  And

And though this firme hereditatry good
Might boasted be as flowing with the blood,
Yet he ne're graspt this stay : but as those, who
Carry perfumes about them still, scarce doe
Themselves perceive them, though anothers sence
Suck in the exhaling odour : so he thence
Ne're did perceive he carried this good smell,
But made new still by doing himselfe well.

(fame
To imbalme him then is vaine, where spreading
Supplies the want of spices ; where the name,
It selfe preserving, may for ointment passe,
And he still seen lie coffind as in glasse.
Whiles thus his bud dims full flowers, and his sole
Beginning doth reproach anothers whole.
Coming so perfect up, that there must needs
Have been found out new titles for new deeds.

(let
Though youth and lawes forbid, which will not
Statues be rais'd, or him stand brasen : yet
Our minds retaines this royalty of Kings,
Not to be bound to time, but judge of things
And worship as they merit : there we doe
Place him at height, and he stands golden too.
A comfort, but not equall to the crosse,
A faire remainder, but not like the losse.
For he (that last pledge) being gone, we doe
Not onely loose the heir but the honour too.
Set we up then this boast against our wrong,
He left no other signe that he was young :

And

And spight of fate his living vertues will,
Though he be dead, keep up the Barony still.

Upon the same.

UNequall nature, that dost load, not pair
Bodies with souls, to great for them to bear !
As some put extracts (that for soules may passe,
Still quickning where they are) in frailer glasse ;
Whose active generous spirits scorne to live
By such weak means, and slight preservative :
                                          (day
So high borne minds ; whose dawnings like the
In torrid climes cast forth a full-noon ray ;
Whose vigorous brests inherit (throngd in one)
A race of soules by long succession ;
And rise in their descents ; in whom we see
Entirely summ'd a new born ancestry :
These soules of fire (whose eager thoughts alone
Create a feaver or consumption)
Orecharge their bodies : labring in the strife
To serve so quick and more then mortall life.
Where every contemplation doth oppresse
Like fits of the Calenture, and kills no lesse.
Goodnesse hath its extreams as well as sin,
And brings, as vice, death and diseases in.

                                          This

This was thy fate, great *Stafford*; thy fierce speed
T'out-live thy years, to throng in every deed
A masse of vertues; hence thy minutes swell
Not to a long life, but long Chronicle.
Great name (for that alone is left to be
Call'd great; and tis no small nobility
To leave a name) when we deplore the fall
Of thy brave Stem, and in thee of them all;
Who dost this glory to thy race dispence,
Not known to honour, e'end with innocence;
Me thinks I see a spark from thy dead eye
Cast beams on thy deceas'd Nobility.
Witnesse those Marble heads, whom *Westminster*
Adores (perhaps without a nose or eare)
Are now twice raised from the dust, and seem
New sculpt againe, when thou art plac'd by them,
When thou, the last of that brave house deceast,
Hadst none to cry (our brother) but the Priest:
And this true riddle is to ages sent
Stafford is his Fore-fathers monument.

A Song

A Song of the Precise Cut.

With face and fashion to be known
  For one of sure election,
With eyes all white and many a groan,
With neck aside to draw in tone,
With harp in's nose or he is none.
  See a new teacher of the town,
  O the town, O the towns new teacher.

With pate cut shorter then the brow,
With little ruffe starcht you know how,
With cloak like Paul, no cape I trow,
With Surplesse none, but lately now;
With hands to thump, no knees to bow.
  See a new teacher, &c.

With couzning cough and hallow cheek
To get new gath'rings every week,
With paltry change of and to eke,
With some small Hebrew, and no Greek,
To find out words when stuff's to seek.
  See a new teacher, &c.

With

With shopboard breeding and intrusion,
With some outlandish Institution,
With *Ursines* Catechisme to muse on,
With *Systems* method for confusion,
With grounds strong layed of meer illusion.
   See a new teacher, &c.

With rites indifferent all damned,
And made unlawfull if commanded,
Good works of Popery down banded,
And morall Lawes from him estranged,
Except the Sabbath still unchanged.
   See a new teacher, &c.

With speech unthought, quick revelation,
With boldnesse in predestination,
With threats of absolute damnation,
Yet yea and nay hath some salvation
For his own Tribe, not every-Nation.
   See a new teacher, &c.

With after licence cost a Crown
When Bishop new had put him down,
With tricks calld repetition,
And doctrine newly brought to town
Of teaching men to hang and drown.
   See a new teacher, &c.

With flesh-provision to keep lent,
With shelves of sweetnesse often spent,

                      Which

Which new maid brought, old Lady sent,
Though to be saved a poor present;
Yet Legacies assure the event.
   See a new teacher, *&c.*

With troops expecting him at door
That would hear Sermons and no more,
With Noting-tools and sighs great store,
With Bibles great to turne them ore
While he wrests places by the score.
   See a new teacher, *&c.*

With running text, the nam'd forsaken,
With for and but both by sence shaken,
Cheap doctrines forc'd, wild uses raken,
Both sometimes one by mark mistaken,
With any thing to any shapen.
   See a new teacher, *&c.*

With new wrought caps against the Cannon
For taking cold, though sure he have none,
A Sermons end when he began one,
A new houre long when his glasse had run one,
New use, new points, new notes to stand on.
   See a new teacher, *&c.*

L   *Upon*

Upon the Lady Paulets *Gift to the*
University of Oxford : *Being an exact piece*
of Needle-work presenting the whole sto-
ry of the Incarnation, Passion, Re.
surrection, and Ascension of
our Saviour.

COuld we judge here most vertuous Madam :
    then
Your needle might receive praise from our pen.
But this our want bereaves it of that part,
Whilst to admire and thank is all our Art,
The work deserves a Shrine : I should rehearse
Its glory in a story, not a verse.
Colours are mix'd so subtilly, that thereby
The strength of art doth take and cheat the eye :
At once a thousand we can gaze upon,
But are deceiv'd by their transition.   (beam
What toucheth is the same ; beam takes from
The next still like, yet differing in the extream.
Here runs this tract, thither we see that tends,
But cannot say here this or there that ends.
Thus while they creep insensibly we doubt
Whether the one pours not the other out.

                           Faces

Faces so quick and lively, that we may
Fear if we turn our backs theyl steal away.
Postures of griefe so true, that we may swear
Your artfull fingers have wrought passion there.
View we the manger, and the Babe, we thence
Believe the very threads have innocence.
Then on the Crosse, such love, such griefe we find
As twere a transcript of our Saviours mind :
Each parcell so expressive, each so fit,   (writ.
That the whole seems not so much wrought as
Tis sacred text, all we may coat, and thence
Extract what may be press'd in our defence.
Blest Mother of the Church, be in the list
Reckond with th' four a she Evangelist ;
Nor can the stile be prophanation, when
The needle may convert more then the pen.
When faith may come by seeing ; and each leafe
Rightly prus'd, prove Gospell to the deafe.
Had not that *Hellen* haply found the crosse
By this your work, you had repaired that losse.
Tell me not of *Penelope*, we do
See a web here more chast and sacred too.
Where are ye now O women, ye that sow
Temptations labouring to expresse the bow
Of the blind Archer : ye that rarely set
To please your loves a *Venus* in a net ?
Turne your skill hither, then we shall no doubt
See the Kings daughter glorious too without.
Women sewed onely figleaves hitherto,
Eves nakednesse is onely cloath'd by you.

On the same.

MAdam, your work's all miracle, and you
The first Evangelist, whose skillfull clue
Hath made a road to *Bethlem*, now we may
Without a stars direction find the way
To the cratch our Saviours cradle, there him see
Mantled in hay, had not your piety
Swath'd him in silk; they that have skill may see
(For sure tis prickt) the Virgins lullaby.
The Oxe would faine be bellowing did he not fear
That at his noyse the Babe would wake and hear.
And as each passage of his birth's at strife
To excell, so even the death's drawn to the life.
See how the greedy souldiers tug to share
His seamelesse coat, as if your work they'd tear :
Look on his read, thats naturall, on his gown
Thats a pure scarlet; so acutes his crown,
That he who thinks not they are thorns indeed,
Would he were prick'd untill his fingers bleed.
His Crosse a skilfull joyner cannot know,
(So neat tis fram'd) where it be wood or no :
So closely by the curious needle pointed,   (ted.
Had *Joseph* seen't he knew not where were joyn-
His side seems yet to bleed and leave a stain,
As if the blood now trickled from the vein :
Methinks I hear the Thiefe for mercy call,
He might have stole't, 'twas nere lock'd up at all.

                                        See

See how he faints ; the crimſon ſilk turns pale
Changing its graine. Could I but ſee the vaile
Rent, all were finiſh'd, but thats well forborn ;
Twere pitty ſuch a work as this we're torn.
Turn but your eye aſide and you may ſee
His penſive handmaids take him from the tree,
Embalming him with tears, none could expreſſe,
Madam, but you death in ſo fit a dreſſe ;
No hand but yours could teach the needles eye
To drop true tears, unfeignedly to cry.
Follow him to his virgin tomb, and view
His corps inviron'd with a miſcreate crue
Of drowſie watch, who look as though they were
Nere bid to watch and pray, but ſleep and ſwear :
The third day being come, and their Charge
Only ſome Relicks left upon the ſtone ;   (gone,
One quakes, another yawnes, a third in haſt
To run had not your needle made him faſt :
And to excuſe themſelves all they can ſay
Is that they dream'd ſome one ſtole him away :
You, Madam, by the Angels guidance have
Fouud him againe ſince he roſe from the grave.
So zealous of his company, no force
Could part you had not heaven made the divorſe ;
Where he remains till the laſt day, and then
I wiſh with joy you there may meet again.

L 3

On

On the same.

Lady,

YOu have drawn, and are all graces; none so
      true
As those lodge in your needle-work and you:
Hither will throng we know these draughts to see
Whole bevies of Court Maddams; such as be
Fair spectacles themselves, yet shall these glasses
Ravish by shewing not theirs but your faces:
Eyes that will shame the Christalls, and outsteal
The patterns quaintest lustre those conceal:
Fingers of Ivory that will pointing stand
As Indexes to shew where moved the hand,
And in what method; till a dawning light (white;
Spread on the Pictures from their neighbouring
Yet so they shall not weave new beauties in
Those webs, your silk is whiter then their skin:
Tis said that some will chang their own for bought
Locks, so they be not painted but thus wrought:
And scanning well these tresses well died threads
Curle into locks about the female heads,
So neatly periwig'd, will choose to wear
Rather what you so make then what grows bair.
This Lady learns a smile from hence, she there
A devout griefe takes forth from *Maryes* tear,
So lively dropt; as if ith' woman 'twas
Water, what's silk ith' needle, pearl ith' glasse.

A

A third will imitate your selfe, and try
Each pieces counterfeit : which being set by
As types unto your Gospel, all will guesse
You are the Evangelist, she the Prophetesse.

Here lies my Saviour ; and though he it is
Lends life to all, yet borrows he from this:
And doth to th' world by two Nativities come
Both from your fancy and from *Maryes* womb
For who observes the Art will move a strife
Whether the threads be more of silk then life.
All things are in such proper colours shown ;
The naturall seem feigned, these their own :
And all so well compos'd, their juncture such,
It were some seperation but to touch :
As in the varied bow which Heaven bends
The red appears and yet the blew nere ends ;
Here green, and yellow there, yet none can see
Where green or yellow do begin to be,
Each into others transient, and so fit
Still, what you choose nothing would serve but it.
What punctuall thorns here crown the Crucifix;
I thought your needle, but your silk more pricks.
The sides wound had appeared by a cleft
Ith' wound; had you but so much unwrought left
And open; as through which the spear once stole,
Now you have fill'd it 'tis a truer hole.
Did you pin down the hands and feet twould fail
Much of the truth, the stich is verier naile:
Well drops the blood in shadow; were there need
Of true, but squeeze the Picture and 'twould bleed:

For

For life that onely floats in vainer breath
Other arts give : that which returns from death :
Yours fresh and fully ideates , and is one
That holds out to a Refurrection.
Here tis that it to Chrift joyntly procures
A rifing from both bottomes, hell and yours :
His countenance refin'd feems not more new
Iffuing out from the grave then from your clew ;
Allmoft fo much of the Diety is fhown
In your works as is vifible in its own :
In thefe materialls we may more God fee
Then heathens in a flower, or a true tree.
But could we reach your fancy and find in't
The fpirituality of every Print ;
We darkly might conceive pure Godheads, one
Nature, our Chrift both of his flesh and bone.
Bleft Soule, who thus internally haft eyed
Thy Saviour ; how haft thou been fanctified ?
I dare to fay fo long as he ftayed in
Your minds, pure mirrour, that you fcarce did fin:
Had but one idle thought difturb'd the glaffe,
That fame reflected blemifh would forth paffe
Into the ftained table, and no doubt
The blur within had been a blot without.
Look ore the Paffion ; now you only view (new.
Old wonnds ; had you then finn'd you had made
But all is acurate : we cannot find
One fault in the copy, caufe not one ith' mind :
And yet tis drawn in fuch briefe Imagry
The fmalleft error cannot unfeen lye.

Each

Each picture's couched in so little space,
Had you but miss'd a thread y'had lost a face.
Not as in gouty Arras, where a list
Of any colour if left out's not mist,
And where the shuttle twenty times mishot
Makes not so rude a sphalm, as here a knot
Or stich let faln : tis easie to excell
Where's such a latitude of doing well.
But, Madam, you that in two Tables draw
The Gospell whole, as God wrought all the Law,
Are both compendious and true : the story
Doth something loose in bulk, nothing in glory.
The Magi are made lesse, but not lesse wise,
Their gifts diminish, but their values rise :
For since they are come hither, thats thought best
Which they do bring from you, not from the East.
We cannot pen forth all your Art, much lesse
Our Obligations and our thanks expresse :
More will be said when we can better prize
Your Present : mean while (Lady) let this suffice.

With such delight we your Imbrodry view,
No other object can please more but you ;
Whose gift hath swoln us to such thankfull pride
W'have now no matter for a wish beside
The giver ; you alone outvy it, and
Wee'l wave the work onely to kisse your hand.

Against

Against
BEN: *JOHNSON.*

1.

COme leave that saucy way
Of baiting those that pay
Dear for the sight of thy declining wit :
   I know it is not fit
That a sale-Poet (just contempt once thrown)
   Should cry up thus his own.
   I wonder by what dower,
   Or patent you had power
From all to rape a judgement ? let it suffice
Had you bin modest, y'had bin counted wise.

2.

   Tis known you can doe well,
   And that you can excell
As a translator ; but when things require
   A genius and a fire
Not kindled heretofore by others pains,
   As oft you have wanted brains
   And art to strike the white,
   As you have leveld right :
But if men vouch not things Apocriphall,
You bellow, rave, and spatter round your gall.

Iugge,

3.

Jugge, Peg, Pierce, Fly, and all
  Your jefts fo nominall,
Are things fo far below an able braine,
  As they doe throw a ftaine
Through all the unlucky plot, and doe difpleafe
  As deep as *Pericles* :
  Where yet there is not laid
  Before a chamber-maid
Difcourfe fo weak, as might have ferv'd of old
For **Schoolboys** when they of love or valor told.

4.

  Why rage then when the fhow
  Should judgement be ; and know
That there are thofe in **Plufh** that fcorn to drudg
  For **Stages**, yet can judge
Not onely **Poets** loofer laws but wits,
  With all their perquifits :
  A gift as rich and high
  As noble **Poefy**,
Which though in fport it be for Kings a play,
Tis next Mechanick when it works for pay.

6.

Alcæus Lute had none,
  Nor loofe *Anacreon,*
That taught fo bold affuming of the baies
  When they deferv'd no praife.

                    To

To raile men into approbation
  Tis new ; tis yours alone ;
  And prospers not. For know
  Fame is as coy, as you ;
Can be disdainfull ; and who dares to prove
A rape on her shall gaine her scorne not love.

6.

  Leave then this humerous vaine,
  And this more humerous straine,
Where selfe conceit and choler of the blood
  Eclips what else is good :
Then if you please those raptures high to touch
  Whereof you boast so much,
  And but forbear the crown
  Till the world put it on :
No doubt from all you may amazement draw,
Since braver theam no *Phœbus* ever saw.

Upon

Upon a Gentlewoman who broke her vow.

WHen first the Magick of thine eye
    Usurp'd upon my liberty,
Triumphing in my hearts spoile, thou
Didst lock up thine in such a vow :
When I prove false may the bright day
Be governd by the Moons pale ray :
And I too well remember, this
Thou saidst and sealdst it with a kisse.
O heavens ! and could so soon that tie
Relent in slack Apostasie ?
Could all thy oaths and morgag'd trust
Vanish like letters form d in dust,
Which the next wind scatters ? take heed,
Take heed, Revolter, know this deed
Hath wrong d the world ; which will fare worse
By thy example then thy curse.
Hide that false brow in mists thy shame ;
Nere see light more, but the dim flame
Of funerall lamps : thus sit and moane
And learn to keep thy guilt at home ;
Give it no vent. For if again
Thy love or vowes betray more men;

At

At length I fear thy perjur'd breath
Will blow out day and waken death.

A Song upon a Winepot.

ALl Poets Hippocrene admire,
And pray to water to inspire
Their wit and muse with heavenly fire.
Had they this heavenly fountaine seen,
Sack both their muse and wit had been,
And this Pintepot their Hipocrene.

Had they truly discovered it,
They had like me, thought it unfit
To pray to water for their wit :
And had ador'd Sack as divine,
And made a Poet God of Wine,
And this Pintepot had bin the Shrine.

Sack unto them had bin instead
Of Nectar and the heavenly bread,
And every a boy a Gannemed :
But had they made a God of it,
Or stiled it Patron of their wit,
This Pintepot had bin a Temple fit.

Well

Well then companions ift not fit,
Since to this gem we owe our wit,
That we fhould praife the Cabinet;
And drink a health to this divine
And bounteous palace of our Wine ?
Die he with thirft that doth repine.

To one married to an old man.

SEeing thou wouldft (bewitch'd by fome ill
Be buried in thofe monnmental arms (charms)
All we can wifh is may that earth be light
Upon thy tender limbs, and fo good night.

A Song.

I Mean to fing of *Englands* fate,   (Mate)
(God bleffe in th' mean time the King and his
Thats rul'd by the Antipodian ftate,
                    Which no body can deny.

Had thefe feditious times been when
We had the life of our wife Poet *Ben,*
Apprentices had not been Parliament men,
                    Which no body can deny.
                                        But

But Puritans bear all the sway ;
And they'l have no Bishops as most of them say,
But God may have the better another day,
                    Which no body can deny.

Prin and *Burton* say women that are lewd and
Shall wear Italian locks for their abuse,   (loose
They'l onely have private keys for their own use,
                    Which no body can deny.

Zealous *Prin* hath threatned a shrewd downfall
To cut off long locks both bushy and small,
But I hope he will not take eares and all,
                    Which no body can deny.

They'l not alow of what pride in brings,
No favours in hats nor any such things,
They'l convert all ribbands into Bible strings,
                    Which no body can deny.

God blesse the King, and Queen also,
And all true Subjects from high to low,
TheRoundheads can pray for themselvesweknow,
                    Which no body can deny.

                                        Upon

Upon the Times.

THe *Parliament* cries arme, the *King* says no ;
The new *Lievtenants* cry on, lets go ;
The *People* all amaz'd, ask where's the foe ?
The bugbear *Scots* behind the door cry boh.
Patience a while, and time will plainly shew
The *King* stands still faster then they can goe.

A double Chronogram (*the one in
Latine the other in the English of that
Latine*) *upon the year* 1642.

TV DeVs IaM propItIVs sIs regI regnoqVe
hVIC VnIVerso.

O goD noVV sheVV faVoVr to the kIng
anD thIs V.VhoLe LanD.

M   On

On the Noble-mans Sons Cloak
that refused to wear a Gown in Oxford.

SAw you the Cloak at Church to day
The long-worne fhort Cloak lined with Say ?
What had the Man no Gown to wear,
Or was this fent him from the Mayor ?
Or ift the Cloak which Nixon brought
To trim the Tub where Colledge taught ;
Or can this beft conceal his lips,
And fhew Communion fitting hips ?
Or was the Cloak St Pauls ? if fo
With it he found the Parchments too.
Yes verily ; for he hath been
With mine Hoft Gajus at the New-Inn.
A Gown (God bleffe us) trailes oth' floore
Like th' petticoat of the Scarlet Whore ;
Whofe large ftiffe pleats he dares confide
Are ribs from Antichrifts own fide.
A mourning Cope, if 't looks to the Eaft,
Is the black Surpliffe of the Beaft.
Stay, read the Cards ; the Queens and Kings
The beft ith' Pack are Gouned things ;
But fhort cut Spade with t'other three
Are dub'd ith Cloak of knavery.
Befide his Lordfhip cloak'd did ftand
When his Watch went falfe by flight of hand :
Then look for more fuch Cloaks as thefe
From th' Court of Wards and Liveries.

On

On Alma's voyce.

WHat Magick art
Compells my soule to fly away,
And leave desert
My poor composed trunck of clay?
Strange violence ! thus pleasingly to teare
The soule forth of the body by the eare.

When *Alma* sings,
The pretty Chanters of the skie
Doe droop their wings,
As in disgrace they meant to die;
Because their tunes which were before so rare.
Compar'd to hers, doe but distract the aire.

Each sensitive
In emulation proudly stands,
Striving to thrive
Under the blisse of her commands, (tame,
Whose charming voyce doth Bears and Tigers
And teach the Sphears new melodies to frame.

The Angells all
(Astonisht at her heavenly aire)
Would sudden fall
From cold amazement to dispaire;
But that by nimble theft they all conspire
To steal her hence for to enrich their quire.

F I N I S.

Appendix

Five pages (reduced in size) from Abraham Wright's miscellany *Excerpta quaedam per A.W. adolescentem* compiled *c.*1640 (British Library, Additional MS 22608, ff. 83v–85v) including his extracts from, and comments on, Shakespeare's *Othello* and *Hamlet*.

Out of _____ of Othello. By Shakespeare.

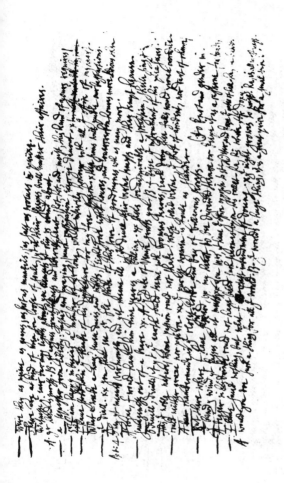

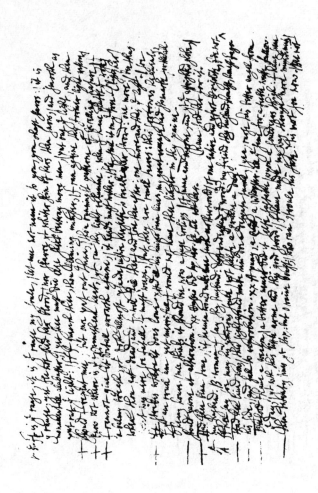

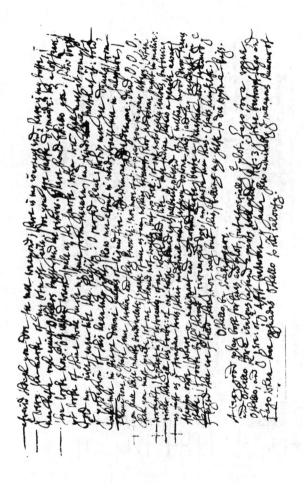

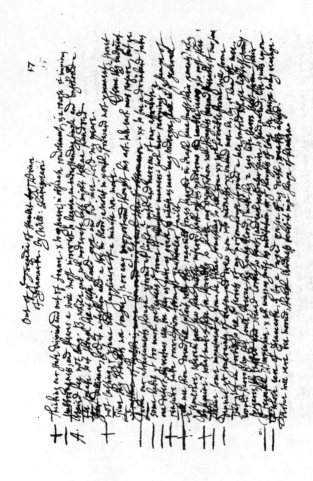

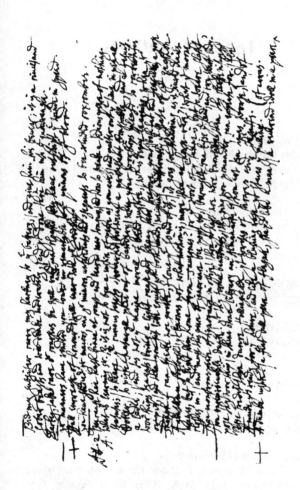

Index of Authors

page

Baker, William
possibly the chaplain to Archbishop Abbot, *fl.*1618–29, but there were other William Bakers at the universities, one at the Middle Temple in 1606

75, 97 *bis*

Blount, Sir Henry (1602–82)
educ. St Albans School; Trinity College, Oxford (*matric.* 1615, B.A. 1618); Gray's Inn, 1620; knighted 1639. Traveller

64

Bond, William (? *b.* 1617/18)
educ. Christ Church, Oxford (*matric.* 1636)

134

Bristol, Earl of
see Digby

Brome, Alexander (1620?–66)
Royalist poet and dramatist

110

Brome, Richard (*c.* 1590?–1652/3)
servant to Ben Jonson, *c.* 1614. Dramatist

57

Browne, William (1590?–1645?)
educ. Tavistock grammar school; Exeter College, Oxford, *c.* 1603 (*matric.* 1624, M.A. 1625); Inner Temple, from Clifford's Inn, 1611; later attached to household of Herbert family, Earls of Pembroke. Poet

Carew, Thomas (1594/5–1640)
educ. Merton College, Oxford (*matric.* 1608, B.A. 1611);
Middle Temple, 1612; diplomatic appointments in Italy,
The Hague and Paris, 1613–19; Gentleman of the Privy
Chamber, 1628, and subsequently Sewer in Ordinary to the
King
70

Carey, Thomas (1597–1648/9)
second son of Robert Carey, first Earl of Monmouth; *educ.*
Exeter College, Oxford (*matric.* 1611, B.A. 1614);
Gentleman of the King's Bedchamber
120

Cartwright, William (1611–43)
educ. Westminster School; Christ Church, Oxford, 1628
(*matric.* 1632, B.A. 1632, M.A. 1635); Proctor, 1643. Poet,
dramatist and divine
45, 59, 136, 137, 146

Corbett, Richard (1582–1635)
educ. Westminster School; Broadgates Hall [Pembroke
College], Oxford (*matric.* 1598); Christ Church, Oxford,
1599 (B.A. 1602, M.A. 1605, D.D. 1617); Proctor of Christ
Church, 1612; Dean of Christ Church, 1620; Bishop of
Oxford, 1628–32; Bishop of Norwich, 1632-5
18, 46, 47, 48, 65, 81, 82, 84, 112, 115

Dalby, Edward (*b.* 1614/15)
educ. New College, Oxford (*matric.* 1634); Wadham
College, Oxford (B.A. 1635); Inner Temple (barrister 1641)
148

Digby, John, first Earl of Bristol (1580–1654)
educ. Magdalen College, Oxford, 1595 (M.A. 1605); Inner
Temple, 1598; Gentleman of the Privy Chamber, 1605;
knighted 1606; Vice-Chamberlain of the Household, 1616–
25; created Baron Digby 1617 and Earl of Bristol 1622.
Diplomatist and statesman
161

Donne, John (1573–1631)
educ. Hart Hall, Oxford (*matric.* 1584, M.A. 1610; D.D. at Cambridge 1615); Lincoln's Inn, 1592; Secretary to Sir Thomas Egerton, 1597/8; Royal Chaplain; Reader at Lincoln's Inn, 1616–22; Dean of St Paul's, 1621–31; vicar of St Dunstan's in the West, 1624

64, 86, 97 *bis*, 118

Earles, John (1600/1–65)
educ. Christ Church, Oxford (*matric.* and B.A. 1619); Merton College, Oxford (Fellow 1619, M.A. 1624, D.D. 1642); Proctor of Christ Church, 1631; member of Great Tew circle; tutor and chaplain to the future Charles II, 1641; Dean of Westminster, 1660; Bishop of Worcester, 1662–3; Bishop of Salisbury, 1663–5

12, 40

Felltham, Owen (1602?–68)
author

154

Gawen, Thomas (1612–84)
educ. Winchester School, 1625; New College, Oxford (Fellow 1632–41, B.A. 1634, M.A. 1639). Writer and divine; Roman Catholic convert

150

Godfrey, Richard (1618/19–49)
educ. Christ Church, Oxford (*matric.* 1637, B.A. 1641, M.A. 1647)

141

Goodwyn, Thomas (1589/90–1644)
son of Francis Goodwyn, Bishop of Llandaff; *educ.* Christ Church, Oxford (*matric.* 1604, B.A. 1608, M.A. 1611, D.D. 1621); Canon of Llandaff, 1613; Canon of Hereford, 1619; Chancellor of Hereford Cathedral, 1624

24

Grange, John (? *b.* 1586/7)
educ. Balliol College, Oxford (*matric.* 1604); Lincoln's Inn, 1604

66

Halswell, Henry (*fl.* 1602–9)
educ. Christ Church (*matric.* 1602), St Edmund's Hall (B.A. 1605) and All Souls College, Oxford (M.A. 1609)
101

Harris, John (? *b.* 1600/1)
educ. Christ Church, Oxford (*matric.* and B.A. 1621)
18

Harvey, Martin (? *b.* 1610/11)
educ. Christ's College, Cambridge (*matric.* 1627, B.A. 1630); Middle Temple, 1629
124

Herrick, Robert (1591–1674)
apprenticed to uncle, the King's Jeweller, 1607; *educ.* St John's College, 1613–16, and Trinity Hall, Cambridge (B.A. 1616; M.A. 1620); chaplain on Isle of Rhé expedition, 1627; rector of Dean Prior, Devon, 1629/30–46, 1660–74
'96'

Holland, Abraham (*d.* 1626)
son of the translator Philemon Holland; *educ.* Trinity College, Cambridge, 1614 (B.A. 1616/17). Poet
16

Jonson, Ben (1572–1637)
educ. Westminster School under William Camden; honorary degree at Christ Church, Oxford, while guest of Richard Corbett, 1619. Dramatist
29

King, Henry (1592–1669)
eldest son of John King, Bishop of London; *educ.* Westminster School; Christ Church, Oxford (*matric.* 1609, B.A. 1611, M.A. 1614); prebendary of St Paul's, 1616; honorary member of Lincoln's Inn, 1619; Royal Chaplain to Charles I and Charles II; Dean of Rochester, 1639; Bishop of Chichester, 1642–3, 1660–9.
30, 70, 80, '91' [90], 157

L'Estrange, Sir Roger (1616–1704)
   educ. possibly at Cambridge; fought for Royalists in Civil
   War. Tory pamphleteer and licenser of the press after the
   Restoration

107

Lewis, William (1577–1667)
   educ. Hart Hall, Oxford (B.A. 1608); Oriel College,
   Oxford (Fellow 1608; M.A. 1612, D.D. 1627); chaplain to
   Francis Bacon; Provost of Oriel College, 1618–22; chaplain
   and secretary to the Duke of Buckingham on Isle of Rhé
   expedition, 1627; Royal Chaplain; Master of the Hospital
   of St Cross, Winchester, 1628–43, 1660–7

32

Mayne, Jasper (1604–72)
   educ. Westminster School; Christ Church, Oxford, 1623
   (B.A. 1628, M.A. 1631, B.D. 1642, D.D. 1646); Canon of
   Christ Church, 1660; Archdeacon of Chichester under
   Henry King, 1660–72. Poet, playwright and divine

40, 129

Morley, George (1598–1684)
   educ. Westminster School; Christ Church, Oxford, 1615
   (B.A. 1618, M.A. 1621, D.D. 1642); member of Great Tew
   circle; Canon of Christ Church, 1641; Royal Chaplain;
   Dean of Christ Church, 1660; Bishop of Worcester, 1660–2;
   Bishop of Winchester, 1662–84

'92' [91], '93' [92], '94' [93]

N., N.

158

Poole, Walton
   ? of Gray's Inn, London, 1611

75

Randolph, Thomas (1605–35)
   educ. Westminster School; Trinity College, Cambridge
   (*matric.* 1624, B.A. 1628, minor fellow 1629, major fellow
   1632, M.A. 1632). Dramatist and poet

43

Reynolds, Henry (*c.* 1564–1635)
held court posts with the Master of the Revels and Lord Chamberlain, 1606–13; schoolmaster, *c.*1614–32. Poet, author and translator
'91' [90]

S., W.
75

Shirley, James (1596–1666)
educ. Merchant Taylors' School, 1608–12; St John's College, Oxford, 1612; Catharine Hall, Cambridge (B.A. 1618); apprenticed to a scrivener, *c.*1612–15; lived in Gray's Inn, *c.* 1624, and became member, 1634; later in retinue of Earl (afterwards Duke) of Newcastle. Dramatist; Roman Catholic convert
36, 97 *bis*

Stone, Benjamin (*b.* 1584/5)
educ. New College, Oxford (*matric.* 1605, B.A. 1609)
22, 23

Strode, William (1602–45)
educ. Westminster School; Christ Church, Oxford, 1617 (*matric.* 1621, B.A. 1621, M.A. 1624, B.D. 1631, D.D. 1638); chaplain to Richard Corbett, 1628; Public Orator of Oxford University, 1629–45; Canon (1638) and Sub-Dean of Christ Church, 1639–43. Poet and dramatist
31, 39, 67, 68, 72, 74, 77, 83, 100, 104, 114, 117, 143

Vaughan, Sir John (1603–74)
educ. the King's School, Worcester; Christ Church, Oxford, 1623; Inner Temple, 1620; called to the Bar, 1630; Bencher, 1660; knighted 1668; Deputy Speaker of Commons, 1669–70. Lawyer and politician
82

Waller, Edmund (1606–87)
educ. Eton College; King's College, Cambridge (*matric.* 1621); Lincoln's Inn, 1622; M.P. intermittently 1624–87. Poet and politician
159

Wild, Robert (1615/16–79)
    educ. St John's College, Cambridge, 1632 (B.A. 1636, M.A. 1639, D.D. 1660; B.D. of Oxford 1642). **Puritan divine, poet and Royalist**

63

Wotton, Sir Henry (1568–1639)
    educ. Winchester School; New College, Oxford (*matric.* 1584); Queen's College, Oxford (B.A. 1588); Middle Temple, 1595; Provost of Eton College, 1624–39. **Diplomatist**

34

Wright, Abraham (1611–90)
    educ. Merchant Taylors' School; St John's College, Oxford (*matric.* 1629, Fellow 1632, B.A. 1633, M.A. 1637). **Divine**
                        1, 54, 121, 122, 126, 128

Index of Titles

page

Against Ben: Johnson   154
Aged gentlewoman, On an   118
Aglaura Printed in Folio, Upon   57
Alma's voyce, On   163
Answer to the Letter of the Cloake, An   134
Answer, The   66

Barclay his Epitaph   '95' [94]
Bell-Founder of great Tom of Christ-Church in
    Oxford, To the   115
Ben: Johnson To Burlace   29
Bible, On the   31
Black Gentlewoman, On a   75
Black Gentlewoman Mistresse A.H., To a   128
Black maid to the faire boy, The   '91' [90]

Catholick, The   83
Copy of Verses spoke to King Charles by way of
    entertainment when he was pleas'd to grace S.
    John's Colledge with his visit. 1636, A   121

Death of a faire Gentlewomans Robin-redbrest, On
    the   71
Death of Prince Henry, Upon the   30
Death of Sir Tho: Pelham, On the   72
Death of the Lord Stafford, the last of his name, Upon
    the   137

Double Chronogram (the one in Latine the other in
   the English of that Latine) upon the year 1642, A   161
Dr. Griffith heald of a strange cure by Bernard Wright
   of Oxford, To   104
Dr. Langton, On   114
Dr. Price writing Anniversaries on Prince Henry, To   46
Dr. Ravis Bishop of London, On   112

Earle of Pembroke's Death, On the   40
Elegie, Upon the death of Sir John Burrowes, Slaine
   at the Isle of Ree, An   12
Epitaph on some bottles of Sack and Claret laid in
   sand, An   63

Faire gentlewomans blistered lip, On a   67
Faireford windowes, On (I know no paint of Poetry)   84
Faireford windows, On (Tell me you anti-Saints . . .)   81
Fortunes Legacy   124

Gentleman, that kissing his Mistresse left blood upon
   her, On a   117
Gentlewoman playing on the Lute, On a   82
Gentlewoman that had the Small-Pox, On a   67
Gentlewomans entertainment of him, Upon a   126

Heavens best Image, his faire and vertuous Mistresse
   M.S., Upon   88
His Answer   '91' [90]
His chast Mistresse, Upon   43
His imperious Mistresse, To   110
His Mistresse, To (Ile tell you how the Rose . . .)   75
His Mistresse, To (Keepe on your mask . . .)   68
His Mistresse eye, On   102
His Mistresse going to Sea, On   120
How to choose a Mistresse   64

Journey into France, A   24

Kings Book bound up in a Cover coloured with His
   Blood, Upon the   54
Kings Returne to the City of London when he came
   last thether from Scotland and was entertained
   there by the Lord Mayor, Upon the   50

Ladies Attire, On   65
Lady Paulets Gift to the University of Oxford: Being
   an exact piece of Needle-work presenting the whole
   story of the Incarnation, Passion, Resurrection,
   and Ascension of our Saviour, Upon the   146
Lady that dyed of the small pox, On a   48
Letter to his Mistresse, A   39
Liberty and Requiem of an imprisoned Royalist, The   107
Love, On   82
Lover to one dispraising his Mistresse, A   70
Loves Courtship   136

Man, On   80
Memory of Ben: Johnson, To the   129
Mr. Hammon Parson of Beudly For pulling down the
   May-pole, To   18
Mr. Hoptons death, Upon   101
Mr. Sambourne, sometime Sherife of Oxford-shire,
   On   22
Musick, Of   74

New Quadrangle of St. John's Colledge in Oxford,
   built by the most Reverend Father in God the Lord
   Archbishop of Canterbury, Upon the   122
Nightingale, The   '94' [93]
Noble-mans Sons Cloak that refused to wear a Gown
   in Oxford, On the   162
Nuptials of John Talbot Esquire, and Mistresse
   Elizabeth Kite, Upon the   55

Ode in the praise of Sack, An   60
Of Musick   74

On a black Gentlewoman   75
On a faire Gentlewomans blistered lip   67
On a Gentleman, that kissing his Mistresse left blood
     upon her   117
On a Gentlewoman playing on the Lute   82
On a Gentlewoman that had the Small-Pox   67
On a Gentlewoman walking in the Snow   77
On a Lady that dyed of the small pox   48
On a Painters handsome Daughter   45
On a white blemish in his Mistresse eye   16
On a woman dying in travell the child unborne   79
On Alma's voyce   163
On an aged Gentlewoman   118
On Dr. Langton   114
On Dr. Ravis Bishop of London   112
On Faireford windowes (I know no paint of Poetry)   84
On Faireford windows (Tell me you anti-Saints . . .)   81
On his Mistresse eye   102
On his Mistresse going to Sea   120
On Ladies Attire   65
On Love   82
On Man   80
On Mr. Sambourne, sometime Sherife of Oxford-shire   22
On the Bible   31
On the death of a faire Gentlewomans Robin-redbrest   71
On the death of Sir Tho: Pelham   72
On the Earle of Pembroke's Death   40
On the Noble-mans Sons Cloak that refused to wear
     a Gown in Oxford   162
On the praise of an ill-favour Gentlewoman   86
On the Princes birth   36
On the same [Lady Paulet's gift]   148
On the same [Lady Paulet's gift]   150
One dead in the Snow, Upon   78
One married to an old man, To   159

Painters handsome Daughter, On a   45
Paradox on the praise of a painted face, A   97 *bis*

Picture, Upon a 64
Poem, In defence of the decent Ornaments of
  Christ-Church Oxon, occasioned by a Banbury
  brother, who called them Idolatries, A 3
Praise of an ill-favour Gentlewoman, On the 86
Princes birth, On the 36

Reply upon an Answer to the former Copy, A 47

Same, On the [Lady Paulet's gift] 148
Same, On the [Lady Paulet's gift] 150
Same, Upon the [the death of Lord Stafford] 141
Sheriffs Beere, Upon the 23
Sir Henry Wotton on Q: Elizabeth 34
Some pieces of work in York House, Upon 32
Song of the Precise Cut, A 143
Song upon a Winepot, A 158
Song, A (I mean to sing of Englands fate) 159
Song, A (When Orpheus sweetly did complain) 100

Temper. Upon Dr. Juxon Bishop of London, The 1
Times, Upon the 161
To a black Gentlewoman Mistresse A.H. 128
To Dr. Griffith heald of a strange cure by Bernard
  Wright of Oxford 104
To Dr. Price writing Anniversaries on Prince Henry 46
To his imperious Mistresse 110
To his Mistresse (Ile tell you how the Rose . . .) 75
To his Mistresse (Keepe on your mask . . .) 68
To Mr. Hammon Parson of Beudly For pulling down
  the May-pole 18
To one married to an old man 159
To the Bell-Founder of great Tom of Christ-Church
  in Oxford 115
To the Memory of Ben: Johnson 129

Upon a Gentlewoman who broke her vow 157
Upon a Gentlewomans entertainment of him 126

Upon a Picture   64
Upon Aglaura Printed in Folio   57
Upon Heavens best Image, his faire and vertuous
   Mistresse M.S.   88
Upon his chast Mistresse   43
Upon Mr. Hoptons death   101
Upon one dead in the Snow   78
Upon some pieces of work in York House   32
Upon the death of Prince Henry   30
Upon the death of the Lord Stafford, the last of his
   name   137
Upon the Kings Book bound up in a Cover coloured
   with His Blood   54
Upon the Kings Returne to the City of London when
   he came last thether from Scotland and was
   entertained there by the Lord Mayor   50
Upon the Lady Paulets Gift to the University of
   Oxford: Being an exact piece of Needle-work
   presenting the whole story of the Incarnation,
   Passion, Resurrection, and Ascension of our
   Saviour   146
Upon the new Quadrangle of St. Johns Colledge in
   Oxford, built by the most Reverend Father in God
   the Lord Archbishop of Canterbury   122
Upon the Nuptials of John Talbot Esquire, and
   Mistresse Elizabeth Kite   55
Upon the same [the death of Lord Stafford]   141
Upon the Sheriffs Beere   23
Upon the Times   161

Venus lachrimans   59
Verses sent to a Lady which she sending back unread,
   were returned with this inscription   '92' [91]
Verses, The   '93' [92]

Welcome to Sack, A   '96' [95]
White blemish in his Mistresse eye, On a   16
Woman dying in travell the child unborne, On a   79

Index of First Lines

	page
A beauty smoother than the ivory plain	67
All poets Hippocrene admire	158
Am I once more blessed with a grace so high	102
And now more great than when you were	1
As when the vestal hearth went out no fire	129
Be silent you still music of the spheres	82
Beat on proud billows Boreas blow	107
Because of fleshly mould we be	114
Behold this little volume here enrolled	31
Behold those fair eyes in whose sight	64
Black Cypress veils are shrouds of night	66
Black girl complain not that I fly	'91' [90]
Blind fortune if thou want'st a guide	124
By this large margent did the poet mean	57
Come grand Apollo tune my lyre	55
Come leave that saucy way	154
Could we judge here most virtuous madam then	146
Did not my sorrows sighed into a verse	40
Enter and see this tomb sirs do not fear	63
Even so dead Hector thrice was triumphed on	46
Fair boy alas why fliest thou me	'91' [90]
Farewell fair saint may not the seas and wind	120

Fie scholars fie have you such thirsty souls   22

Go happy paper by command   39
Great sir and now more great than when you were   1
Grief's prodigals where are you? unthrifts where?   101
Grieve not fair maid 'cause you are black so's she   128

Hark my Flora love doth call us   136
He that's imprisoned in this narrow room   '95' [94]
Hear me as if thy ears had palate Jack   60
Her for a mistress would I fain enjoy   64
Hide not your sprouting lip nor kill   67

I hold as faith   83
I know no paint of poetry   84
I'le tell you how the rose did first grow red   75
I mean to sing of England's fate   159
I saw fair Chloris walk alone   77
I went from England into France   24
I wonder that you should send for the cloak   134
If shadows be a picture's excellence   75
If there be haply any man that dares   16
Ill busied man why shouldst thou take such care   80
In those fair cheeks two pits do lie   69

Keep on your mask and hide your eye   68
Keep station nature and rest Heaven sure   30

Lady you have drawn and are all graces none so true 150
Let abler pens commend these leaves whose fame   54
Love give me leave to serve thee and be wise   43

Madam your work's all miracle and you   148
Marry and love thy Flavia for she   86
Merely for death to grieve and mourn   72
Mr Roberts I wonder that you should send for the
    cloak   134
Must then our loves be short still? must we choose   137

My limbs were weary and my head oppressed   '94' [93]

No spring nor summer's beauty hath such grace   118
Nor is it grieved grave you the memory   47
Not kiss? by Jove I must and make impression   97 *bis*

Oh God now show favour to the King and this whole
     land   161
Oh thou deformed unwomanlike disease   48
Oh wound us not with this sad tale forbear   12
On a day 'tis in thy power   '93' [92]
Our Oxford sheriff of late is grown so wise   23

Read fair maid and know the heat   '92' [91]

Saw you the cloak at church today   162
Seeing thou wouldst bewitched by some ill charms   159
Sing and be merry King Charles is come back   50
So soft streams meet so streams with gladder
     smiles   '96' [95]
Such are your father's pictures that we do   45

Tell me you anti-saints why glass   81
The mighty zeal which thou hast late put on   18
The most insulting tyrants can but be   88
The Parliament cries arm the King says no   161
Thou that by ruin dost repair   115
'Tis done and now where's he that cried it down   122
Tu Deus iam propitius sis regi regnoque huic universo   161

Unequal nature that dost load not pair   141

View this large gallery faced with mats and say   32

Wake my Adonis do not die   59
Welcome abroad oh welcome from your bed   104
Well fare the Muses which in well chimed verse   36
Well well 'tis true   110

Were they not angels sang did not mine ears 121

What magic art 163

What mystery is this that I should find 117

Whatsoe're birds in groves are bred 71

When first the magic of thine eye 157

When I do love I would not wish to speed 82

When I passed Paul's and travelled on the walk 112

When Orpheus sweetly did complain 100

When whispering strains with creeping wind 74

Whether sweet mistress I should most 126

Why slight you her whom I approve? 70

Why though I be of a prodigious waist 29

With face and fashion to be known 143

Within a fleece of silent waters drowned 78

Within this grave there is a grave entombed 79

Ye glorious trifles of the east 34

You have drawn and are all graces none so true 150

You ladies that wear Cypress veils 65

You that profane our windows with a tongue 3